Writing Effective Lesson Plans

The 5-Star Approach

PETER SERDYUKOV

National University

MARK RYAN

Walden University

Boston • New York • San Francisco
Mexico City • Montreal • Toronto • London • Madrid • Munich • Paris
Hong Kong • Singapore • Tokyo • Cape Town • Sydney

To Natasha

Executive Editor and Publisher: Stephen D. Dragin
Series Editorial Assistant: Katie Heimsoth
Marketing Manager: Weslie Sellinger
Production Coordinator: Mary Beth Finch
Composition Buyer: Linda Cox
Manufacturing Buyer: Linda Morris
Electronic Composition: Denise Hoffman
Interior Design: Denise Hoffman
Cover Administrator: Linda Knowles

For related titles and support materials, visit our online catalog at www.ablongman.com.

Between the time website information is gathered and then published, it is not unusual for some sites to have closed. Also, the transcription of URLs can result in typographical errors. The publisher would appreciate notification where these errors occur so that they may be corrected in subsequent editions.

ISBN 10: 0-205-51149-X
ISBN 13: 978-0-205-51149-5

Library of Congress Cataloging-in-Publication Data

Serdyukov, Peter.
   Writing effective lesson plans : the five star approach / Peter Serdyukov, Mark Ryan.
       p. cm.
   Includes bibliographical references and index.
   ISBN 978-0-205-51149-5 (alk. paper)
1. Lesson planning.   I. Ryan, Mark, 1947–   II. Title.

LB1027.4.S47 2008
371.3'028—dc22

                                                                2007007183

Printed in the United States of America

10 9 8 7 6 5 4 3 2   [CIN]   11 10 09 08

Lesson plans in Appendix D used by permission of Columbia Education Center, Portland, OR.

About the Authors

Peter Serdyukov has been a professional educator for 35 years. He has been involved in teacher preparation for the last 25 years. He holds a PhD in Applied Linguistics from Kiev State Pedagogical Institute of Foreign Languages and a Degree of Doctor of Pedagogical Sciences from Kiev State Linguistic University, Ukraine. Dr. Serdyukov is currently a Professor in the Teacher Education Department at National University, La Jolla, CA. He is author or co-author of 17 books and over 80 book chapters, articles, and scientific papers.

Mark Ryan has taught at all grade levels, from elementary classes to university seminars. He holds a Bachelor's degree in history from the University of California at Santa Cruz, a Master's degree from the University of Puerto Rico at Rio Piedras, and a Doctorate in Higher and Adult Education from Arizona State University at Tempe. From 1994 through 1997 he wrote the *Ask the Teacher* column syndicated by Copley News Service and was regularly published in such newspapers as the *Boston Herald*, the *Denver Rocky Mountain News*, and the *San Diego Union Tribune*. In 2004 Dr. Ryan received the President's Distinguished Teaching Award from National University. One of his books, *Ask the Teacher: a Practitioner's Guide to Teaching and Learning in the Diverse Classroom* can be found in over 200 universities worldwide.

Contents

Preface

Consistent effective lesson planning is essential for successful experiences in both teaching and learning. In teacher preparation, the most important goal is to prepare an educator for quality teaching in the classroom. Quality teaching, like any other occupation, requires sound rational planning, organization, and management. One of the prerequisites for achieving this goal is the teacher's competence in lesson plan design which becomes an important objective in every practitioner's professional development.

Lesson planning is essential in almost every aspect of daily classroom life. Good lesson plans are the foundation of successful student learning, accurate assessment, and effective classroom management. Every teacher, at some point, needs guidelines for designing quality lessons. Initial guidance in lesson plan development followed by instructional practice is the key to successful teaching.

Traditionally, planning skills have not been sufficiently developed in the teacher preparation programs or in the classroom experiences. Novice and even seasoned teachers, on being involved in the lesson planning activities, often note their lack of planning skills in the previous educational experiences. This is why there is an urgent need to have a text that effectively guides lesson plan development. This book combines concise and clear theoretical explanations with practical activities that help enhance user skills in designing and developing lesson plans. This text can be used by every teacher in daily practical work as a one-stop resource for designing lesson plans that encourage deep and thoughtful learning, in teacher life-long professional development and certainly in teacher education college courses preparing future teachers for rewarding classroom experiences.

To aid in developing your 5-Star Lesson Plan, see the list of Internet sites below containing state standards for all 50 states. Each state updates its Internet sites as new standards are approved. The following are Web sites the authors found useful:

- www.education-world.com/standards/state/index.shtml
- http://edstandards.org/Standards.html
- http://promethean.statestandards.com/

Acknowledgments

The authors would like to acknowledge Dr. Ralph Nelsen of the Colombia Education Center, who generously gave us permission to use adaptations of the Center's lesson plans for our text; Dr. Donald Kauchak, University of Utah, for valuable advice and evaluation; our colleagues at National University, who have been successfully using the materials that laid the foundation of this book in their teaching, especially Dr. Robyn Hill and Ronazae Adams, National Board Certified Teacher; and our students, who were the first to test our approach in lesson planning and gave exciting feedback for text improvement. We would also like to thank the following reviewers for their helpful comments: Mary F. Leslie, Louisiana State University at Eunice; Nancy Brashear, Azuza Pacific University; and Carol Marra Pelletier, University of Massachusetts, Dartmouth.

CHAPTER 1

Structure and Stages of Development

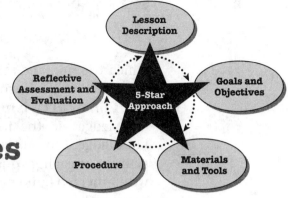

*B*efore the first students come through the classroom door, a teacher must be prepared to begin the learning process based on a plan of action. This chapter will define a lesson plan, examine the rationale for planning, indicate the stages of lesson plan development, and describe the sequencing of lesson components. A well-thought-out lesson plan gives the teacher a sense of direction and may well foster a feeling of confidence and enthusiasm in implementing instruction, thereby setting an atmosphere for learning.

Coming to Terms over Defining and Designing a Plan

A **plan** is a systematic means to reach an end. Quality teaching, like any other occupation, requires rational and sound planning, organization, and management. One of the prerequisites for achieving this goal is the teacher's competence in lesson plan development. Planning therefore becomes an important part of every practitioner's professional development.

Lesson planning is essential in almost any aspect of daily classroom life. Good lesson plans are the foundation of successful student learning, accurate assessment, and effective classroom management. Every teacher, at some point, needs clear guidelines for designing quality lessons. Lesson plan development followed by instructional practice is a key to successful teaching. A well-structured plan might, in a sense, mirror a rational approach due to its clear and concise format. Nevertheless, the authors accept a constructivist view of learning in which the sum and substance of the learning experience is ultimately controlled by the learner.

Constructivism is based on the notion of building up one's own knowledge via the interaction between prior knowledge and new knowledge. It is an ongoing process of gathering new knowledge and actively engaging, questioning, problem solving, and collaborating with others to build new meanings. Because we traditionally learn in a social environment we also collaboratively build a common knowledge that will eventually be interiorized by each member of the learning community individually. Lesson planning is about learner engagement in activities that provide for knowledge construction and skill development.

So, What Is a Lesson Plan?

A **lesson plan** is a model of organized learning events within a standard time period of a formal instructional process. Constructed by a teacher, it determines the structure and sequence of the teaching and learning activities to be performed during that period. Both the teacher and students will perform these planned activities intended to achieve the learning goals and specific objectives of the lesson.

A lesson plan is a projection of a real lesson, a structure filled with concrete processes, assignments, and learning tools. Moreover, it usually includes everything necessary for the lesson implementation, such as: teaching/learning materials, activity banks, visuals, handouts, and technological applications. So, a lesson plan is actually a model of the lesson to be taught in the future.

A lesson plan is a blueprint on which to construct a learning process made up of clearly stated goals and objectives, which research has shown (Gronlund 2000) enhances student outcomes. Accordingly, clear and well-organized structure to obtain information promotes superior retention as compared to a less organized information model (Fuchs et al. 1997). Communicating *in advance* via a lesson plan what the students are to achieve permits a teacher to devise reflective assessments and evaluations to measure student progress.

Finally, a lesson plan is a tool that moves from theory to practice (effective lesson plans are based on the most up-to-date educational research) by carrying out a methodological approach structured enough to ensure clear and concise direction, yet flexible enough to provide for differentiation to meet the needs of every student.

Stages of Lesson Plan Development

Lesson planning is a specific teacher activity focused on designing and developing a practical model and procedure for future lessons. There are four main areas of planning: *preparation, development, implementation* and *reflection.*

PREPARATION

Who is to be taught? For instance:

- Selecting the relevant content responsive to the learner's needs by investigating his or her prior knowledge and individual characteristics (i.e., their "cultural toolbox") and identifying their learning needs so as to achieve the desired outcomes.

● WHAT'S THE PLAN?

Identify the needs of English Language Learner (ELL) students:

_____

_____

_____

_____

Identify the needs of special education students:

_____

_____

_____

_____

Identify the needs of high-achieving students:

_____

_____

_____

_____

Identify the most essential needs of your whole class:

_____

_____

_____

_____

DEVELOPMENT

What is to be taught? For instance:

- Lesson's instructional goals
- Specific learning objectives
- State standards
- Concepts
- Content
- Life skills

● WHAT'S THE PLAN?

As you approach the stage of developing a lesson plan, think of the difference between teaching concepts and content. (**Hint:** *Note the distinction between teaching concrete and abstract subject matter.*)

_____

_____

_____

_____

IMPLEMENTATION OF INSTRUCTIONAL METHODOLOGIES

How do you usually teach students? For instance, which are your favorite methodological approaches?

- Direct instruction
- Collaborative learning (group or team work)
- Self-directed learning
- Peer tutoring

What instructional tools and strategies do you use?

- Lesson structure and design
- Materials and technology applications
- Instructional procedures and activities
- Reflective evaluation and assessment tools and techniques

● WHAT'S THE PLAN?

How are you going to teach your content area topic? (***Hints:*** *lecturing a class from the textbook, offering students the opportunity to independently search for the information on the topic on the Internet, dividing them into small groups and giving them handouts, asking them to prepare presentations for the class, or other teaching strategies.*)

_____

_____

_____

_____

_____

_____

REFLECTION

The fourth and final area of planning is reflection. This is where you analyze the strengths and weaknesses of your lesson plan both before implementing it in the classroom and after. For instance, before the lesson: Does your plan adequately prepare all students for new curricular content? Are your goals and objectives in line with state standards? Do you have the needed materials and tools to carry out the lesson plan? Are the activities in your procedures geared to accommodate different learning styles? Are you specifically assessing and evaluating knowledge and/or skills that relate to your aforementioned goals and objectives? Have you designed a lesson that is culturally responsive? After the lesson: Have you achieved the planned goal and objectives? Did student learning outcomes meet the expectation? What worked and what did not, and how you could have done better? John Dewey (Dewey 1938) once remarked that learning is not merely acquiring information, but making that learning relevant to our everyday life.

● WHAT'S THE PLAN?

Describe how you might revise or enhance the activities component of your lesson plan to better facilitate the learning process and thus increase your enthusiasm in teaching the lesson and your confidence as a teacher.

_____

_____

_____

_____

_____

Lesson Plan Designs

There are different ways to design a lesson plan: a narrative, a bullet format, a block scheme, or an algorithm (a step-by-step procedure that often involves repetition).

A narrative is convenient for a beginning teacher who may prefer to have everything written out. It looks like a script of a play where everything is written: what the teacher does and says and what the students are supposed to do. For example:

> In the beginning of the lesson, I will ask students some questions in order to identify what they know about a topic. Then I will read the text during which I will explain to them . . .

This format may seem convenient, but it does not give an explicit structure to the lesson.

A bullet format lists the steps of the lesson, such as "read a text," "ask students questions," "give students assignment," or "have students write their problem solution on the board." For example:

- Ask questions.
- Read text.
- Explain the new words.
- Organize a small group discussion.

This is a frequently used format.

A block scheme presents a lesson structure in a graphic form, thus allowing the teacher to see all the activities to be performed in the lesson in a predetermined sequence and interrelation. In this format, the lesson plan can be presented as a modular structure (Figure 1.1). Each module corresponds to a specific part or phase of the lesson with particular objectives, content, and activities (for example, new material presentation or classroom activities aimed at developing particular skills). A typical lesson plan structure includes the following five components as shown in Figure 1.1.

● **FIGURE 1.1**

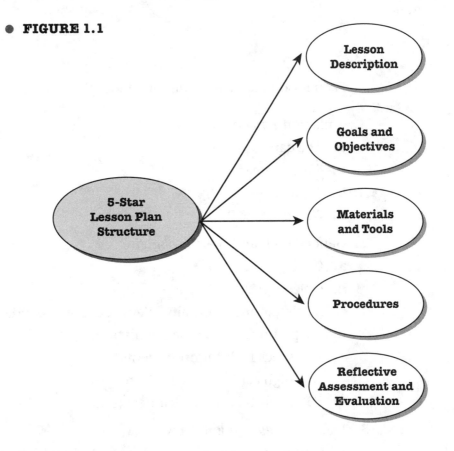

Structuring a Lesson Plan

All effective lesson plans have a structure. Typically, lesson plans follow this structure in writing. Our lesson plan consists of five components. We call this lesson plan the **5-Star Lesson Plan** (Figure 1.2).

Actually, within this standard structure the teacher selects the most useful lesson plan model that responds best to students' learning styles and prior knowledge. Correspondingly, the teacher strives to present the most enriched curriculum using the widest variety of methodological approaches.

● **FIGURE 1.2**

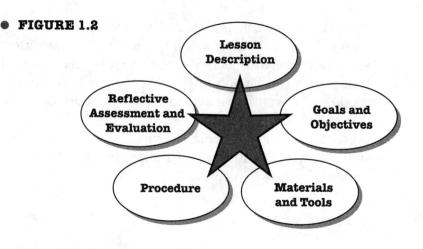

Each lesson plan component includes the following:

1. A plan's *description*
   a. The date
   b. Subject area
   c. Topic
   d. Grade

2. General *goals* and specific *objectives*
   a. Goal
   b. Objectives
   c. Academic and culturally relevant content standards
   d. Adaptations for diverse populations
      i. special education students
      ii. high achieving (gifted) students
      iii. English language learners (ELL)

3. Teacher's *materials* and *tools*
   a. Instructional resources, such as texts, handouts and visuals
   b. Educational technology hardware and software (computer programs, educational games, multimedia)

4. Lesson's *procedure*
   a. Introduction
   b. Content presentation
   c. Activities
   d. Assessment and evaluation
   e. Closure

5. Reflective *assessment* and *evaluation*

    a. Lesson reflection and assessment (via observations and conferences between students and the teacher)

    b. Evaluation (tests, quizzes and essays)

Note: A **5-Star Lesson Plan** is typically implemented in a five-step procedure (Figure 1.3).

● **FIGURE 1.3**

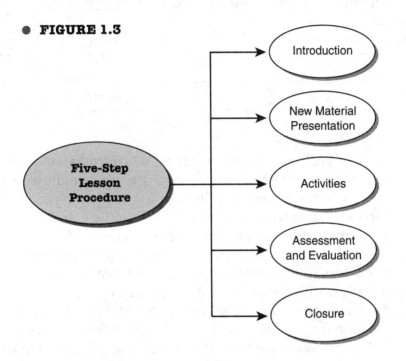

A Generic Lesson Plan

A generic lesson plan is a typical structure accepted for designing a lesson. A 5-Star Lesson Plan consists of five parts:

1. Description

2. Goals and objectives

3. Materials and tools

4. Procedures

5. Assessment and evaluation

The description contains all the essential information about the lesson plan: the date of the lesson, subject area, topic, grade, goals and objectives, standards, and rationale. If may also include the teacher's name and general class characteristics, such as the number of students, their developmental level, the number of ELLs and their ESL proficiency, special education and gifted students.

● WHAT'S THE PLAN?

What lesson plan format adaptations might you employ, depending on your audience?

_____

_____

_____

The goals and objectives are set when the rationale for the lesson is given, including the state content standards and the explanation of why the lesson is important for the learner. In a sense, the lesson plan starts with a statement of goals and objectives, and they permeate all the activities until lesson outcomes are achieved.

It is also useful to point out interdisciplinary connections and academic content standards (state approved standards) and explain to students how this lesson fits into their curriculum. In every lesson, the teacher should always make reference to what is being learned, why it is important for the student, and how it relates to other learning and their own lives. Therefore, the learner should be aware of the relevance of a specific knowledge, skill, or activity. The general demeanor of a caring and competent teacher is essential at this stage of the lesson to set an environment where students can choose to become motivated, one that will lower the students' level of anxiety and enhance learning and subsequent achievement.

● WHAT'S THE PLAN?

Do you know where to find your state's standards? (***Hint:*** *Just go on the Internet and view your State department of education. Standards are posted; bookmark the site and write the address below.*)

_____

_____

_____

The materials and tools are the instructional resources and technological hardware and software the teacher needs to present, implement, and measure the efficacy of a given lesson plan. Video or multimedia, in addition to printed text and images, can be very effective presentation tools. The lesson plan normally includes a list of materials and other teaching and learning resources, as well as technology applications.

For example, teaching and learning materials, books, visuals (charts, pictures, slides, posters), manipulatives, and realia make up some of your options. Also critical to the contemporary classroom is educational technology in terms of hardware (overhead projectors, computers, DVD players) and courseware (overhead transparencies with images or text, videos and computer software—educational programs and games and PowerPoint slides). You have to select among the available tools those that will best serve your lesson objectives. *Recall:* How you present new information will affect how students will understand and retain it.

● WHAT'S THE PLAN?

What instructional tools do you use to make your presentation of new material more effective and motivational? (**Hint:** *Think of visuals, projectors, video, multimedia, and PowerPoint.*)

_____

_____

_____

_____

_____

The procedures to work through a lesson plan usually include five steps:

- Introduction
- New material presentation
- Student activities
- Assessment and evaluation
- Closure

Students need to be engaged in the lesson at every step:

- When the previously learned information is reviewed
- When new material is presented
- When students perform various activities based on the lesson material

This engagement is necessary to assure understanding, construct new knowledge, provide retention and support skill development.

Introduction is the initial part or phase of the lesson, intended to prepare students for learning by warming up, "setting the stage," general conversation, reviewing the previous lesson's key points, and finding out what prior knowledge the students may have. It may also include checking homework.

New material presentation is the phase where the teacher introduces the fresh information in the form of an expository lecture or a narrative or by reading from a text. Often the teacher uses various visuals germane to the area of study. Presentation may be enhanced by educational technology applications, such as slides, video clips, multimedia shows, and PowerPoint demonstrations.

Students can at times make presentations if they have been given a home assignment to search for new information or develop a project and present it in the class. The presentation phase is extremely important, as it sets the model from which the students will learn.

Student activities include various assignments that can be done individually or collaboratively, among which are Q&A, exercises, case studies, problem solving, role playing, discussions, presentations, and demonstrations. These activities may be of at least two levels of complexity, basic (guided exercises) and advanced (independent practice).

The difference between these levels is as follows: Basic activities are to be accomplished according to patterns or simple models, with little flexibility in their implementation and managed by the teacher. This is done on purpose because the objective here is to develop initial skills, simulating or imitating a certain sample and using particular predetermined knowledge. In teaching ESL, for instance, these activities include various language exercises, such as drills, Cloze testing, substitution, multiple choice, and simple communicative activities, such as simulation and role playing.

Advanced activities, on the other hand, are less controlled (some teacher guidance may be helpful, however) and allow for more freedom and flexibility in their implementation. Students are not limited in their performance except by the task, topic, setting, and purpose of the particular activity. Examples of practice are dramatization, real-life simulations, games, and project development.

An important aspect of all activities is the application of new material and skills in real-life or simulated situations, whether it is in the classroom, on the computer, with homework, or in community service.

Assigning homework is a process that entails giving and explaining the assignments to be done at home. These assignments serve as extension activities to reinforce or broaden the content covered and competencies developed. They literally extend the school day. What is important about homework is that students are given creative and useful assignments that are focused not only on providing retention but also on developing specific knowledge and skills.

Here is an example. Compare the two assignments:

Assignment One: "Read the text, do exercises 35 and 37."

Assignment Two: "In the text, find out what the hero was doing on a particular day, try to explain his acts and suggest options and alternative ways to achieve the purpose".

Clearly, assignment two requires a creative approach that would include higher-order critical thinking skills, whereas assignment one is just a formal task.

● WHAT'S THE PLAN?

Now write an assignment for a class in the style and with the substance of assignment two:

_____

_____

_____

_____

_____

Reflective *assessment* and *evaluation* allow us to judge the efficacy of our teaching and student learning. Assessment can be conducted in the form of questions or dialogue between the teacher and the student to determine that student's strengths and weaknesses. Evaluation, which takes the form of a score, grade, or ranking, can be conducted by a written test, examination, or quiz. Remember that checking for understanding is just an initial step in assessing your student's perception and progress.

Assessment can also be integrated in the activities phase when the teacher judges students' performance. Genuine assessments are ongoing and informal, as the teacher is continuously assessing the class as well as each individual student's performance and progress. This requires a teacher to possess both a competent judgment and a caring attitude.

A part of assessment and evaluation is checking up on homework. Students present their assigned out-of-class work, either by making oral presentations or by turning in written work. It is important that the students realize that "we don't do disposable work."

Because corrected homework is never a throwaway exercise, after homework has been corrected and, if need be, revised to be brought up to standard, it should be of high enough quality to be posted on a classroom bulletin board. A classroom full of high-quality student work provides a model that demonstrably meets a high standard. When the bulletin boards are full, old work is taken down and put in a portfolio. This honors the work and provides a qualitative record for teachers, students, parents, and administrators.

The teacher reaches *closure* when the lesson plan has been completed. Closure is then a phase that incorporates the reflective review of the lesson and the summary of the lesson's key points. It also includes a general appraisal (assessment and evaluation) of the students' work and a short preview of the lesson to come.

● WHAT'S THE PLAN?

How is assessment different from evaluation?

_____

_____

_____

_____

_____

_____

Putting It All Together

Now, when each lesson step has been thought out and written down, it is time to put all your preparations together. Keep in mind that there are constant and variable elements in the lesson plan structure. Introduction and closure are constant elements. You should not come into the class and start teaching without greeting the students, smiling, and talking to them, thus preparing them for work. Correspondingly, you should not abruptly interrupt your teaching and students' work when the bell rings. This would be like watching a football game that ends in the 53rd minute. Other components may be added to the plan, depending on concrete goals and circumstances. The lesson can be completely devoted to the activities, but it would hardly be effective to focus the whole lesson only on presenting new information, without reinforcing it with activities.

Such a considered representation of the lesson plan creates a blueprint of what is to be studied that can be implemented in different ways. Once this plan is in place, it is relatively easy to infuse it with relevant content and activities. For example, the teacher can adapt the plan to a particular subject area or to special students' (for example, ELL) needs. The actual structure of your lesson will depend on the goals, objectives, and actual situations in the class. This adaptation may start with teaching a carefully selected new vocabulary, proceed to tapping into students' background knowledge of the topic by questions and informal conversation, and end with playing a short video clip as an introduction to the new material.

● WHAT'S THE PLAN?

How do you think the components of the 5-Star Lesson Plan structure might interact with each other?

_____

_____

_____

_____

_____

_____

What Is in the Lesson Plan?

If we look closely at the 5-Star Lesson Plan, we can find an array of important preparation aspects to consider (Figure 1.4):

- Lesson topic
- Academic standards
- Culturally relevant curriculum
- Goals and objectives
- Projected outcomes
- Student characteristics
- Lesson structure
- Subject matter content
- Degree of specificity (level of complexity)
- Format of new material
- Instructional methods, strategies, and procedures
- Student activities
- Supporting materials and learning tools, including educational technology
- Assessment and evaluation tools and techniques
- Space and time (the latter is always limited; the challenge for the teacher is to use it efficiently)

When you develop a lesson plan, remember to consider the *who, what, how,* and *why* of actual classroom teaching and learning. Fundamentally you are asking, "How can I achieve successful outcomes in my class?"

Sequencing Lesson Components

What is important in the lesson plan is not only the structure of the lesson or the content and the set of activities for a achieving given goal but also their sequence. The main principle in sequencing the learning events in a lesson is multidirectional. The multidirectional principle can set up the events in a lesson from the presentation of new material

● **FIGURE 1.4**

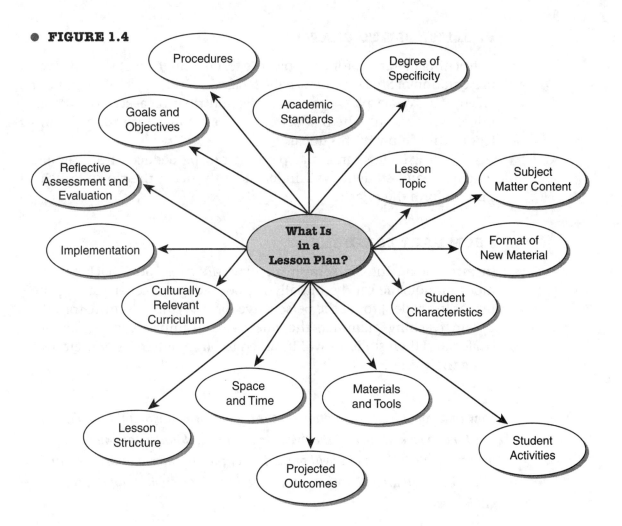

to the assessment and evaluation of learning outcomes. A sequence can develop as follows: introduction (presentation) of the new material, then activities intended to retain the new knowledge and develop appropriate skills, and finally, appraisal of learning outcomes. You shouldn't conduct a comprehensive evaluation before the lesson material is mastered; however, assessment and problem solving can be used at any stage as the students learn course content.

The multidirectional principle also posits that student learning is not commonly unidirectional. Depending on a given student's entry-level characteristics and learning style, the teacher can present material going from the simple to the complex, from the complex to the simple, or from whole to part versus from part to whole. Compare the following two examples.

FROM WHOLE TO PART

In teaching literature, for example, the teacher might first show a video presentation of Shakespeare's *Hamlet*. Based on this (whole) three-hour video of a five-act play, the students could then be asked to write an initial essay on only the first act or only one topic, for instance Hamlet's relationship with his uncle.

In an ESL class, grammar patterns can be deduced from sample sentences, and students will independently make their own conclusions to form the rules.

FROM PART TO WHOLE

In introducing the Shakespearean play *Macbeth*, Lady Macbeth's famous monologue can be initially introduced (by teacher reading the text or in a video) to set the perspective for studying the entire tragedy.

In teaching grammar, the rules with examples can be demonstrated and then students will be asked to build sentences of their own using these rules.

Now that you have a foundation on the overall structure of a lesson plan, it is time to look at each of the five components and understand how they are interrelated. Chapter 2 will present you in-depth information about the 5-Star Lesson Plan description, focusing on the date, subject, topic, and grade level.

C H A P T E R 2

Lesson Description

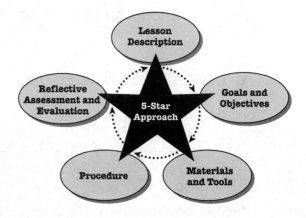

When first approaching the lesson plan, it is important to understand a gestalt of the model. You may well find that the 5-Star Lesson Plan presents a convenient way to conceptualize an overview of a fairly detailed process. Chapter 2 points to the importance of knowing when, what, and to whom you are teaching. Moving from description to goals and objectives to material and tools to procedure and finally to assessment and evaluation, you can view and eventually implement lesson plans to best meet the need of every student.

An Overview of the 5-Star Lesson Plan

Let's begin by designing a lesson plan in your content area for your grade level using the model below by filling in the spaces. Your first try may take a few minutes, but once you become accustomed to the planning process, you will be able to design at a much quicker tempo. When planning, make an approximate projection about how long it may take you to do each activity.

1. DESCRIPTION

Date: _____

Subject: _____

_____

Topic: _____

_____

Grade: _____

2. GOALS AND OBJECTIVES

Goals: Students will learn to:

_____

_____

Objectives: Students will be able to (remember to use action words, such as identify, analyze, critically assess, develop, and demonstrate):

_____

_____

Standards: Content standard (see your state's Web site and copy appropriate standard or standards):

_____

_____

Accommodations for ELL: Consider introducing new vocabulary, grammar points, and modeling pronunciation. Preview major new terms related to the subject and topic. This will be useful for all students, particularly for ELLs preparing for a new content area:

_____

_____

Accommodations for Special Education: Use a wide variety of methodological approaches to meet the needs per specific Individual Educational Plans, with particular emphasis on modes of presentation:

_____

_____

3. MATERIALS AND TOOLS

Texts: _____

_____

Visuals: _____

_____

Technologies: _____

_____

Handouts, Realia, and Manipulatives: _____

_____

_____

4. PROCEDURE

Think of the block of time you have to teach a lesson and then
approximate how many minutes you will need to complete each
of the five steps in the procedure section.

Introduction (_____ min.):

_____

_____

Teacher Presentation (_____ min.): The teacher will:

_____

_____

Class Activities (_____ min.): Students will:

_____

_____

Assessment and Evaluation (_____ min.):

_____

_____

Closure (_____ min.): The teacher will sum up the lesson, naming
the major points discussed.

_____

_____

5. REFLECTIVE ASSESSMENT AND EVALUATION

Assessments (such as conferences) and evaluations (such as testing) are means to judge a student's academic development and/or social growth. Recall that assessments are ongoing dialogues with the learner regarding his or her strengths or weaknesses, while evaluations can be scores, rankings, or grades.

Conferences: _____

_____

Testing: _____

_____

Let's look closely at the first phase of designing a lesson—the description.

Coming to Terms over Description

The lesson description includes basic information about the lesson: the date, subject, topic, and grade (level of study). It precedes the plan itself.

DESCRIPTION

Date: _____

Subject: _____

_____

Topic: _____

_____

Grade: _____

DATE

Although the date describes "when," is also affects "what."

The *date* may seem unimportant in terms of learning theory; after all, we are only considering a given day on the calendar. However, we could probably agree that class dates at the beginning of a school term tend to emphasize introductory materials, while class dates at the end of the term tend to require summative student responses. As you write the date for your class, remember that dates are used to introduce, sustain, and end a sequential learning process.

SUBJECT

Do you think the subject you are assigned to teach is "set in stone" or a foregone conclusion? Think again!

The subject describes the "what," an interdisciplinary subject expands the horizon of the "what." The **subject** being taught most likely refers to a discipline such as English, math, science, physical education, foreign languages, social science, or the performing arts. Sometimes subjects are best taught as interdisciplinary studies. For example, a humanities class can emanate from the combination of a history class (such as American history) and a literature class (such as American literature). Such an arrangement allows teaching a humanities course via thematic units across two traditionally distinct curricula. The advantage is the interrelations and synergy among various areas of knowledge. Whether one chooses to combine content areas (such as math and science) or include an integrated language curriculum—all four language skills in a class (listening, speaking, reading, and writing)—is significant. The choice of how a subject is to be learned is as important as what subject or subjects to study.

● WHAT'S THE PLAN?

What disciplines would you combine in order to integrate the curriculum? (**Hint:** *A math class and a physics class could be combined as a applied science course.*)

_____

_____

_____

_____

_____

TOPIC

The **topic** selected for study is yet another responsibility that has great significance in the learning process. Consider selecting the topics that become projects with both intermediate and long-term goals (for example, writing a sonnet in twelfth-grade English as the first installment in a class collection of poems).

Topics should inform, enlighten, and, if intellectually stimulating, entertain. You might consider topics that grow into projects to provide the kind of developmental format needed to sustain the learning process. One might consider community-based service learning projects that study the effect of local industries on air quality or a multilingual and multicultural poetry festival.

Of course, when choosing topics that become projects, you must decide what is appropriate for learners from preschool through high school in terms of their intellectual development and social growth. It would seem that the best project topics are those that are culturally relevant; have a connection to family, community, and real life; and allow the learner to choose to be inspired, motivated, and ultimately empowered as he or she meets state standards in a learning experience that provides both breadth and depth.

● WHAT'S THE PLAN?

How can you make your lesson more culturally responsive? (***Hint:*** *Think about finding out who your students are and what prior knowledge they bring to class*).

_____

_____

_____

_____

_____

_____

This approach will eventually help our students to meet their ultimate goals of becoming self-directed lifelong learners.

GRADE

Grade level is an organizing principle for schools. Is it always the best way to group students? To sort students by grade is to group. No grouping should be inflexible. Mixed-age and mixed-level groupings can be of great value.

By **grade** we mean a level of study. The most common levels are first grade through twelfth grade. It sounds pretty stable to pass one grade a year and enter another grade the next year. But consider the notion of mixed-age, mixed-level grouping and peer tutoring.

When children of various ages and experiences work together, cognitive restructuring can be facilitated. When a student fails at learning a concept and falls short of the Vygotskian zone of proximal development, the assistance of another student, who can solve problems independently, can support and model the behaviors needed to help the challenged student cross the zone:

> *If you want to learn something better, teach it.*
> (Russian proverb)

If peer tutoring is used, both the participant tutor and the tutee receive benefits. The tutor reinforces what he or she knows, while the recipient gains new insight. In addition, peer tutoring has obvious social growth potential as students reach out to other students to assist in the learning process. So, engage students in cross-grade (cross-age) intellectual interactions whenever there is an opportunity.

● WHAT'S THE PLAN?

Describe an opportunity in the class you are now teaching or plan to teach where peer tutoring could boost academic achievement as well as social growth.

_____

_____

_____

_____

_____

Your Turn: Practice Sheets

Please write out five different description segments of classes you are teaching or plan to teach. Reflect on the options and alternatives you have for date, subject, topic, and grade.

I. DESCRIPTION

Date: _____

Subject: _____

_____

Topic: _____

_____

Grade: _____

II. DESCRIPTION

Date: _____

Subject: _____

_____

Topic: _____

_____

Grade: _____

III. DESCRIPTION

Date: _____

Subject: _____

_____

Topic: _____

_____

Grade: _____

IV. DESCRIPTION

Date: _____

Subject: _____

_____

Topic: _____

_____

Grade: _____

V. DESCRIPTION

Date: _____

Subject: _____

_____

Topic: _____

_____

Grade: _____

Describing the student population you are teaching is the first step to writing an effective lesson plan. Being aware of your students' prior knowledge and of what they need are critical for providing adequate accommodations. This information will allow you to devise a lesson plan to teach the most enriched curriculum via the widest variety of methodological approaches to every student in the class. In the next chapter, you will learn how to write effective goals and objectives that actually define what you are going to accomplish in your lesson.

CHAPTER 3

....

Goals and Objectives

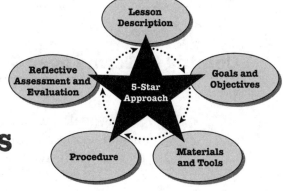

Any lesson has a purpose and an aim. This means every time you teach you should have goals and objectives. This chapter will examine the concepts of goals, objectives, prior knowledge, and standards. Moreover, it will delve into the notion of tangible objectives and the concept of basic vocabulary for any given lesson you may teach. Just like a captain of a ship, knowing where he is going (goal) and what he must accomplish to get there (objectives), you as a teacher must have a firm idea of how to launch a successful lesson plan.

Overview of Goals and Objectives
....

Goals: Students will learn to:

_____

_____

Objectives: Students will be able to:

_____

_____

Standards: _____

_____

Accommodations for ELL and Special Education: _____

_____

_____

Coming to Terms over Goals and Objectives

Setting goals and objectives for your lesson is probably the most critical task in lesson planning. Although as a teacher you may at first believe in your exclusive role in the classroom, understanding the ramifications of students' prior knowledge, learned to a large extent outside the classroom, is crucial to success.

Prior Knowledge

Understanding what students bring to the classroom helps to access their **prior knowledge.** New knowledge begins to be understood when the learner uses his or her prior knowledge to make out familiar patterns of thought within the new knowledge in order to interpret new or enhanced meanings. Within the constructivist framework, prior knowledge is a significant factor in the learning process.

Let's look at a tool you can use in the classroom to access prior knowledge. The K-W-L, created by Ogle (1986), is one way to approach concrete prior knowledge. Learners relate their prior knowledge and engage in the learning process when they state what they *know;* then set goals specifying what they *want* to learn; and after intervening instruction declare what they have *learned.*

Learners make reflective assessments using higher-order critical thinking skills to construct meaning from new information. The worksheet below (Figure 3.1) is a tool that can be given to every learner to ferret out prior knowledge, aspirations, and a reflective assessment of what comprehension has been developed.

● **FIGURE 3.1**

K What I *Know*	W What *Want* to Know	L What I *Learned*

When you, as the teacher, set the goals and objectives, they determine what you expect students to learn and be able to do by the end of this lesson. It is not a very simple task. However, if you do it right, it will help you achieve your aim.

Goals

A **goal** is the strategic, ultimate purpose of the lesson. Goals establish the aim, reason, and rationale for what you and your students will engage in during the lesson. When setting goals, ask yourself where you will take your students and what will you expect them to gain. The goals are typically defined as broad targets related to state or national curriculum standards. For instance: "Students will understand the function of all three branches of government in the United States of America."

● WHAT'S THE PLAN?

Write some goals for a class you are teaching or intend to teach in the future (**Hint:** *Think big as in an encompassing state standard*).

_____

_____

_____

_____

Objectives

An **objective** of a lesson is one of the specific, explicit, intermediate aims that help achieve particular, predesigned outcomes of a lesson. The objectives for a lesson plan are determined by the broader goals of the lesson.

The objectives focus on particular knowledge and skills pertaining to these goals and involve higher-order thinking. To identify the objectives, you should break the goals into a few meaningful interrelated aims or purposes.

> *An objective is a particular intermediate purpose, a component of the overall goal. It assures the student will be able to perform a specific task as a result of the lesson.*

A well-defined objective should be measurable for the learner as well as the evaluator to determine that learning has taken place. Therefore, an objective becomes the criterion for measuring success on reaching an outcome. The action plan is about how to achieve the goals using the objectives as intermediate aims or steps.

There is usually one goal for a particular lesson, (such as "Students will be able to form the plural of nouns," or "Students will be able to explain the location of objects in space," or "Students will demonstrate the ability to divide integers." However, there is usually more than one objective that helps to make the goal attainable. Each objective targets one of the components of the overall goal. For example, for the first of the above-mentioned goals, the objectives might be set as follows:

Students will

- Identify the difference between singular and plural nouns
- Describe *singularia* and *pluralia tantum*
- Explain the grammar rule of forming a plural noun
- Be able to form a plural noun from a singular one
- Demonstrate knowledge and skill in exercises both oral and written

When setting the objectives, ask yourself, "What will students be able to do as a result of this lesson, under what conditions will they accomplish the task, what is the standard of acceptable attainment, and how will students demonstrate what they have learned in the lesson?" (Figure 3.2). To answer these questions, objectives must be specific, tangible, and preferably quantifiable projected outcomes.

● WHAT'S THE PLAN?

Write some objectives for the goal or goals for a class you're teaching or intend to teach in the future (**Hint:** *Check the goal or goals you have already at the beginning of this chapter.*)

_____

_____

_____

● **FIGURE 3.2**

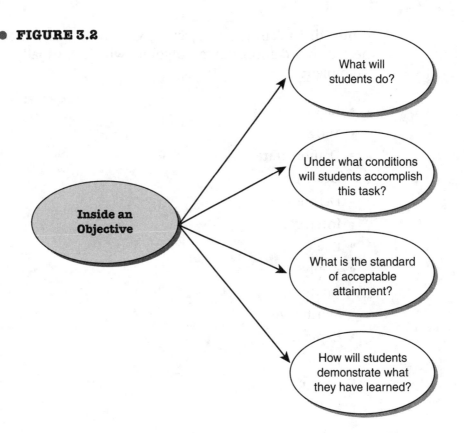

The **outcomes** of the lesson are actually the implemented objectives achieved through effective instruction and students' learning. You strive to enable students to learn to do something concrete and involve higher-order thinking. Therefore you should be very clear in what you expect your students will be able to do as a result of the objectives in this particular lesson.

Having objectives in mind helps you to focus on the right strategies and activities. People often confuse actions with objectives. It is a common mistake to set objectives denoting them as verbs stating what students will do during the lesson, (as in "Students will read, write, present. . . .") These are the procedures described in the lesson, the activities that help to achieve the goals and objectives; however, they are not the purpose, but rather the means of attainment. It is worthwhile to remember that lesson outcomes should match lesson objectives.

> *An objective is a planned outcome.*

Learning objectives in general and behavioral objectives in particular need to be clear, concise, observable, measurable, and student centered. To denote an objective, you should use an action verb connected to a demonstrable outcome, which is usually measurable, for example:

- Identify
- Show
- Demonstrate
- Describe
- Define
- Interpret
- Use
- Apply
- Analyze
- Synthesize
- Explain
- Prove
- Create
- Design

The goals and objectives should be practical and realistic, and they should originate from real-life needs and situations, if possible. For example:

- In an ESL class, we will learn how to order food in a restaurant.
- Students will be able to apply a mathematical formula to save money to purchase a cell phone.

To clearly set the objectives, use Mager's Performance Objectives (Mager 1962) and Bloom's Taxonomy (Bloom et al. 1956). Mager outlines three parts of an objective: Identify the learner, identify the situation in which the learning takes place, and state the criterion for acceptable performance. The taxonomy is helpful for categorizing levels of abstraction of the questions that commonly occur in educational settings.

> *Lesson outcomes should match lesson objectives.*

TANGIBLE Objectives

Objectives should be TANGIBLE. Think of the acronym TANGIBLE when devising your lesson plan. A TANGIBLE objective should: target, acculturate, negotiate, guide, integrate, build, limit, and engage (Figure 3.3).

TARGETS

For example, when a teacher simply states she wants her students to demonstrate their knowledge of U.S. history, there is an obvious lack of specificity as to how that could be accomplished. Students have a much better idea about how to demonstrate their knowledge if the teacher provides options.

> *Possible Objective:* You are president of the United States of America in 1861. The country is on the verge of a civil war. Come up with five realistic proposals for the Congress on how to avoid the bloodshed.

● **FIGURE 3.3**

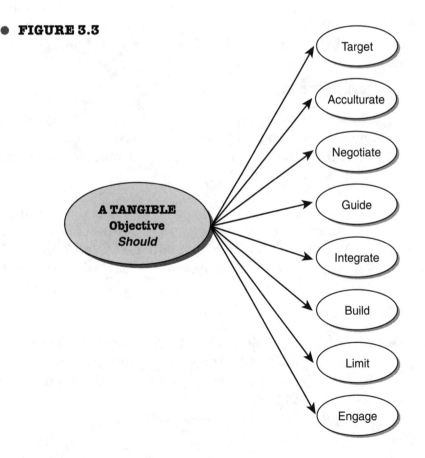

ACCULTURATES

Making connections among contrasting cultural identities that have very different cultural beliefs, communication modes, and interpersonal rapport is essential in a student population ever more culturally and linguistically diverse. Objectives should encourage more team approaches in the classroom so that students could maintain their identity while they learn to appreciate the cultural norms of other classmates.

Objectives need to recognize and endorse multiple identities in students without valuing one identity over another. Objectives can draw on authentic personal experiences while fostering warm relationships with family and community and encouraging students to appreciate and maintain their own cultural heritage as they learn another.

> *Possible Objective:* Interview a family member who was alive during the Vietnam War. Ask that person how the war affected his or her life. Offer a discussion of the topic in the class.

Or:

> Interview a family member or an acquaintance who was not born in the United States and had lived most of her or his life outside this country about how people in that country regarded the United States at that time. Share your findings with the class.

NEGOTIATES

Students should be involved in setting some parts of an objective. People become responsible when they have an opportunity to be accountable. For students to be engaged they must relate in a personal way to what is being taught.

> *Possible Objective:* Do you believe in being healthy? Please share with us your views on this issue: choose whether to write a 1,000-word paper or to deliver a 15-minute PowerPoint presentation on a personal exercise and nutrition plan.

GUIDES

An objective should guide a student through a developmental task via the use of critical thinking skills. Learning progresses to the extent that it takes place via analysis, synthesis, and reflection. Thinking rather than repeating, regurgitating, or parroting is necessary if the objective is to guide the student academically.

Possible Objective: Give your arguments pro or con on capital punishment by participating in a Socratic dialogue. Articulate at least two thoughtful questions or statements about capital punishment within this conversation to demonstrate rigorous thinking as the student moves from the unexamined to examined.

INTEGRATES

An objective should bring together various features of what is to be studied, pointing to meaningful associations with authentic local and global concerns. Objectives should be geared to the real world where the interdependence of knowledge is a reflection of how the brain interconnects reality.

Possible Objective: Students will begin a school rose garden to improve the scenic environment of the community. Students will write a poem about the beauty of the rose garden after the ground area is plotted, the number of plants has been decided, and planting and watering are calculated and assigned.
Note: This objective integrates math, language arts, ecology and service to the community.

BUILDS

An objective should build on the experiences students bring to class. It should also permit students to create or construct their own new understandings or knowledge via a synthesis and special higher-order interaction between the student's previous knowledge and new ideas and/or activities.

Possible Objective: Student teams will build containers to protect an egg to be dropped from a height of 50 feet. Innovative problem-solving approaches and collaboration with other team members are required.

LIMITS

Time and length of an activity are inherently limited because objectives are finite. When you plan a lesson, it is useful to allocate an approximate time to all lesson activities to see if you meet the goals and objectives. Measurements taken of scores or rankings at the completion of a certain objective make up a part of a student's total evaluation.

Possible Objective: Students have one hour to complete ten questions on a short-answer quiz, which is worth 10 percent of their semester grade.

ENGAGES

Student engagement to fulfill an objective is based on motivation. Genuine motivation occurs via student choice. Activities chosen must set an environment where students elect to become inspired, motivated, interested, and ultimately empowered. Recall that unlike a mere incentive, genuine motivation emanates inside a person, providing internal rewards. The staying power of motivation is comparably stronger and more long lasting than that of an incentive (Figure 3.4).

> *Possible Objective:* Students reach out to their community to create a 30-minute concert of holiday songs to sing at children's hospitals in the area.

● WHAT'S THE PLAN?

How does a student become motivated? (**Hint:** *The common notion of a teacher motivating a student is erroneous. What a teacher actually does is set an environment where a student elects to become motivated. So what kind of a classroom environment will lead the student to self-motivate?*)

_____

_____

_____

_____

● FIGURE 3.4

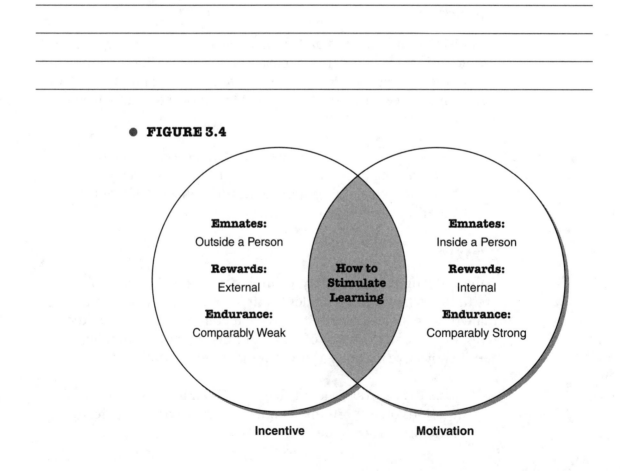

| Incentive | How to Stimulate Learning | Motivation |

Emnates:
Outside a Person

Rewards:
External

Endurance:
Comparably Weak

How to Stimulate Learning

Emnates:
Inside a Person

Rewards:
Internal

Endurance:
Comparably Strong

Incentive   **Motivation**

Standards

An academic **standard** identifies subject area content, which should be aligned with evaluation tools. Academic standards define both breadth and depth. State standards typically delineate anticipated outcomes. In simple terms, they state what students are required to know and what students should be able to perform.

Therefore, standards are not about methodological approaches (the *how* something is done) but are generally discipline specific and therefore curricular and process oriented (the *what*) in nature (Figure 3.5).

> *Standards inform lessons plans and act to gauge academic performance.*

● **FIGURE 3.5**

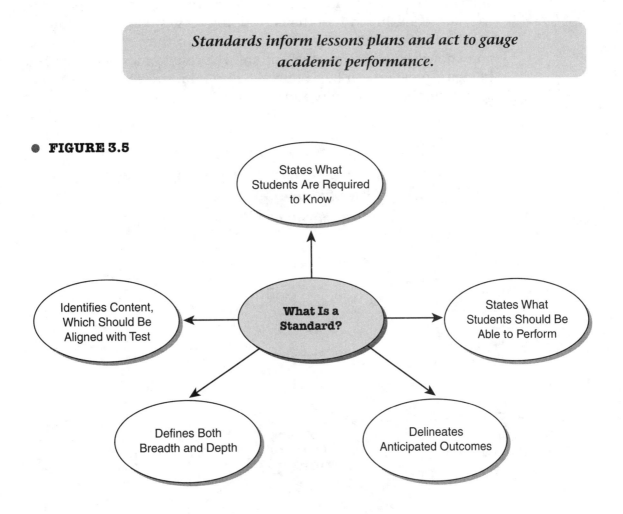

Basic Vocabulary

The idea behind **basic vocabulary** is to make information meaningful to every student by defining ideas and activities via a fundamental terminology. Every student, and ELL in particular, enters school with diverse, culturally based experiences with school and language. Therefore, you can teach vocabulary using English language, integrating learners' first language whenever feasible, and also using visuals, demonstrations, body language, and manipulatives to make the new words comprehensible to all students.

Teaching a basic vocabulary should take into consideration the students' previous experiences to analogize within the process of learning new terms. In terms of the ELL, ideally these students continue to acquire English while they enhance literacy in their native language and knowledge of their native culture. The result of a well-structured bilingual program can be a biliterate, bicultural student who can best serve his or her community and country (Figure 3.6).

> *Research states that reading in one's first language spurs the acquisition of and reading ability in one's second language. Therefore, one can use the first language to accelerate acquisition of the second language.*

● **FIGURE 3.6**

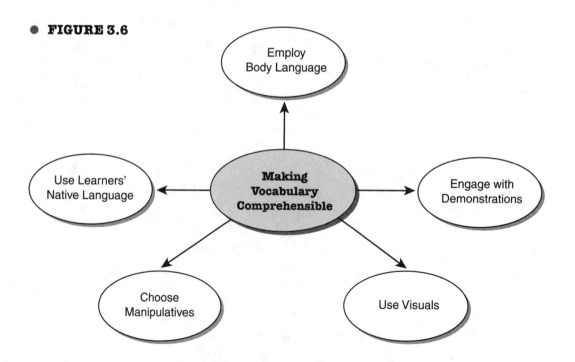

Your Turn: Practice Sheets

Now build the second step of the lesson plan by adding your goals, objectives, and standards to lessons you plan to teach in the future.

I. GOALS AND OBJECTIVES

Goals: _____

_____

_____

Objectives: _____

_____

_____

Standards: _____

_____

_____

Accommodations for ELLs: _____

_____

_____

Basic Vocabulary: Preview major new terms related to the subject and topic. This will be useful for all students, particularly for English Language Learners preparing for a new content area.

_____

_____

II. GOALS AND OBJECTIVES

Goals: _____

_____

_____

Objectives: _____

_____

_____

Standards: _____

_____

_____

Accommodations for ELLs: _____

_____

_____

Basic Vocabulary: Preview major new terms related to the subject and topic. This will be useful for all students, particularly for English Language Learners preparing for a new content area.

_____

_____

III. GOALS AND OBJECTIVES

Goals: _____

_____

_____

Objectives: _____

_____

_____

Standards: _____

_____

_____

Accommodations for ELLs: _____

_____

_____

Basic Vocabulary: Preview major new terms related to the subject and topic. This will be useful for all students, particularly for English Language Learners preparing for a new content area.

_____

_____

IV. GOALS AND OBJECTIVES

Goals: _____

_____

_____

Objectives: _____

_____

_____

Standards: _____

_____

_____

Accommodations for ELLs: _____

_____

_____

Basic Vocabulary: Preview major new terms related to the subject and topic. This will be useful for all students, particularly for English Language Learners preparing for a new content area.

_____

_____

V. GOALS AND OBJECTIVES

Goals: _____

_____

_____

Objectives: _____

_____

_____

Standards: _____

_____

_____

Accommodations for ELLs: _____

_____

_____

Basic Vocabulary: Preview major new terms related to the subject and topic. This will be useful for all students, particularly for English Language Learners preparing for a new content area.

_____

_____

Now that we have reviewed the concepts of goals and objectives, it is time to turn our attention to the resources needed to get the job done. We are specifically referring to materials and tools used by both teacher and students to enhance the learning process. Chapter 4 will present in detail those resources needed to support your lesson plan.

CHAPTER 4

Materials and Tools

From the newest twenty-first-century technology to traditional textbooks, the materials and tools which today's teacher can access provide a wide array of resources to enhance the learning process. In our digital age we can see and hear video via the Internet virtually whenever we want and as many times as we want to reinforce learning. As our tools become more interactive, the role of the teacher does not diminish. As a selector of what web sites to visit and as an assessor of learning, you can explore and access virtually limitless resources in cyberspace.

Overview of Materials and Tools

Lesson Topic: _____

_____

Lesson Goal and Objectives: _____

_____

_____

_____

Texts: _____

_____

_____

Visuals: _____

_____

_____

Technologies: _____

_____

_____

Handouts, Realia and Manipulatives: _____

_____

_____

Coming to Terms over Materials and Tools

Teaching and learning require numerous materials and tools. **Materials** include anything carrying information or used for constructing knowledge and developing skills:

- texts or any other reading materials
- visuals
- drawings
- pictures
- posters
- handouts (ready-made resources to provide content for the activities)
- realia (real-life objects used in classroom activities)
- art and crafts supplies (materials for drawing, coloring, and constructing, such as paper, wood, clay, fabric, and cardboard)
- manipulatives (objects used to build structures, for example, blocks, flash cards, beans)

Tools are teacher and student instruments that can be simple, such as whiteboards, pens, rulers, textbooks, reference books, or more complex (referred to as educational technology) when based on electronics, mechanics, or optics, such as computers, calculators, DVD players, overhead projectors, TVs, computer programs, and the Internet. Materials and tools help enhance learning.

Until recently we thought only about printed text when talking about literacy. Today we also have computer literacy (the ability to operate a computer) and visual literacy (the ability to extract or create meaning from images using electronic devices). Today's students are more accustomed to scanning digital text on the computer screen, hearing digitalized sound in their earphones, and analyzing images on their monitor rather than reading text printed on the paper. Therefore, we have to integrate digital texts, sounds, and images into teaching and learning.

The term **technology** simply means a tool, though a sophisticated one. Just as a knife and fork represent Western technology as eating tools, the computer and the Internet represent learning tools as we look through a monitor and visit informational sites in our journey through cyberspace.

No doubt, the role of electronic technology is growing in society and in the classroom. Newly emergent and more refined devices that relay both sound and image make it important for teachers to consider how technology can enhance the learning process. As we are moving from text-based information to multimedia digital information, we need to use effective ways of information search, selection, evaluation, processing, presenting, and retaining.

Though technology is making teaching and learning more effective, we have to realize technology alone cannot improve what people know or how they learn. It has been said that "a fool with tools is still a fool." Technology can serve the learner well when it is:

- Self-directed (searching the Internet for ideas to bring to science or English class)
- Contextual (watching a video of *Romeo and Juliet* for literature class or a video about Russian czars in a history class)
- Group oriented (producing and directing a school concert via DVD)
- Reflective (using a cell phone or e-mail to send a text message to a fellow math student)
- Informed (checking the class website for assignments and grades)

In all of these activities, technology can encourage the growth of:

- Higher-order thinking skills (analyzing, synthesizing, and evaluating)
- Problem-solving skills (devising solution sets)
- Knowledge construction (building knowledge via interacting with web-based resources and with other people)

- Collaborative learning (working with others to achieve a common goal)
- Instant communication (processing and creating images, text and sound)

Educational Technology Applications in the Lesson

Educational technology (ET) includes technical, programming, and instructional tools used together with human resources in teaching and learning. Technology applications are implemented in the lesson through a research-based set of strategies and techniques to efficiently solve classroom problems emerging in instructional, research, and organizational situations.

Today we use five major groups of ET in instructional practice:

1. *Audio technology:* iPods and DVD and CD players, used to record and play audio text (dialogues, monologues), drama, music, and sounds
2. *Video technology:* DVD, VCR, camcorders, and TV that help to record and play dynamic pictures on video
3. *Projection technology:* slide and overhead projectors, as well as LCD projectors for demonstrating text and images on a large screen
4. *Information and computer technology:* computers with their peripheral devices, such as printers and scanners, that offer computer-based lessons, computer games, virtual reality, multimedia, automated computerized tests, word processors, spreadsheets, databases, graphics, and presentation software
5. *Telecommunications technology:* the Internet, which provides online courses, various distributed Web-based educational resources, Web browers, e-mail, videoconferencing, streaming video, bulletin boards, whiteboards, and chat.

These technologies can be used in all phases of the lesson. They are particularly effective in the presentation phase, in the activities phase, in students' independent work, and in evaluation.

● WHAT'S THE PLAN?

As you develop a lesson plan, think what ETs you might use to make teaching new content more effective. (***Hint:*** *Think what kind of information students will perceive, understand, and retain better due to a particular ET.*)

_____

_____

_____

_____

_____

Teachers who use ET expand the opportunities for productive teaching and learning. You can diversify your methodological approaches via effective content presentation, varied and result-oriented practical activities, access to virtually unlimited Web-based information resources, automated and efficient assessment and evaluation, plus communication capabilities. Technology should be present in teaching and learning whenever the teacher sees an opportunity to enhance the learning environment. Use of ET provides the tools you may need to overcome the context-reduced limitations of the classroom instruction and to set an atmosphere where students have more opportunities to engage in the learning process.

Many of the teaching and learning activities in class, as well as in homework, can be more efficiently performed with ET than without it. You can use ET in the following:

- *Information activities:* information search and processing, for which students can use the computer and the World Wide Web
- *Information presentation:* computer, DVD, CD-ROM, VCR, TV, and projectors
- *Textual activities:* text processing, editing and generating, utilizing text editor or spell check in the computer
- *Learning activities proper:* question-answer, drill, practice, problem-solving, role-playing, and simulation—computer, tape recorder, video camera, VCR, and DVD
- *Communication activities:* dialogue, group discussion, and conference—e-mail, chat, threaded discussion, blog, telephone
- *Evaluation activities:* automated computerized tests

● **W H A T ' S   T H E   P L A N ?**

When preparing a lesson plan, think what kinds of learning activities can be performed in the class when you use ETs. (***Hint:*** *consider student activities you often offer such as: information searching and processing, preparing assignments, communicating and skill development*)

_____

_____

_____

Let us consider a few examples of ET application.

WORD PROCESSOR

The word processor's main use is text generation and processing (Figure 4.1). You can use it as an educational tool for writing instruction, composition skills formation, vocabulary and grammar practice, and project development. Along with developing writing skills, it indirectly helps to develop reading skills as well, due to skill transfer. Working with the text on a word processor helps one stimulate thinking (Figure 4.2).

● **FIGURE 4.1**

● **FIGURE 4.2**

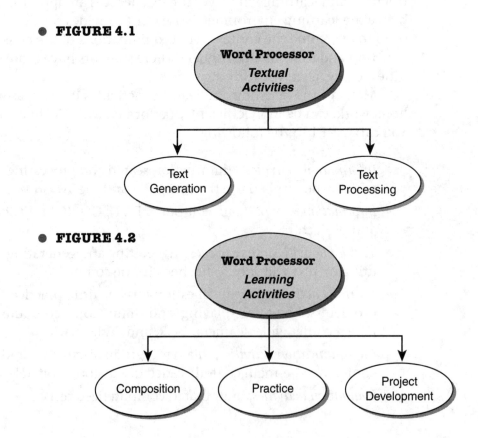

● WHAT'S THE PLAN?

As you develop a lesson plan, think how you can use a computer for students' work with the text. (***Hint:*** *Think about usual activities, such as creating an outline, writing an essay, preparing a report, developing a project, or composing a letter.*)

_____

_____

_____

_____

_____

VIDEO

Video can be used for new material presentation (both in visual and audiovisual formats) and for portraying and simulating real-life situations (Figure 4.3). Activities might include:

- Use video clips to demonstrate models of real-life activities, (for example, shopping, cooking, eating at the restaurant, visiting a doctor, repairing cars, or building houses). These models can help students be more creative in their assignments and projects.

- Use silent video for productive activities, such as describing a realistic situation or writing an audio script in which students write conversations for the actors.

- Demonstrate various communicative situations where native speakers of the language communicate on certain topics. That will give students samples for imitating speech patterns and later for more consistent participation in dialogues and group discussions.

● FIGURE 4.3

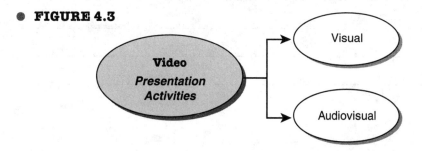

- Show a documentary or a movie on a topic related to the lesson to help connect instruction to real-life situations. Video can be used for content presentation and as material for class activities or homework (such as for writing an essay, discussing an issue, or solving a problem).

Video can be integrated in individual and group learning activities such as problem solving, role playing, simulation games, and group discussions (Figure 4.4). The latter application is particularly important for situated learning when a videotaped real-life situation is used for group analysis and discussion. For example, a video about the rain forest may be used for research and project development, while a video about a French restaurant serves as an excellent model for students learning how to speak French in the dining situations.

● **FIGURE 4.4**

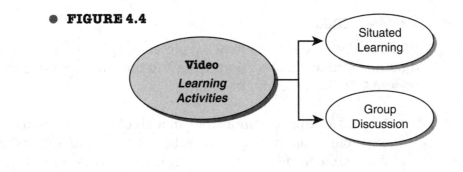

● **W H A T ' S   T H E   P L A N ?**

As you develop a lesson plan, think how you can use video demonstrations to improve your content presentation and upgrade student work. (***Hint:*** *Think about enhancing your lecture or text presentation with video clips or offering students a video for a discussion or problem solving.*)

_____

_____

_____

_____

_____

E-MAIL

E-mail is used predominantly as a communication tool for individual and group message exchange. At the same time, it is a great instrument for reading and writing instruction, tutoring, consultations, question-and-answer exercises, problem solving, and role playing (Figure 4.5). Activities can include:

- Advise students to exchange information for assignments and homework.
- Suggest that students collaboratively develop a project, sharing their individual contributions with the team.
- Establish active e-mail communication in the class so that students create a learning community outside school where they can discuss assignments, their work, problems, and their solutions.
- In an ESL class, get in touch with a class studying English as a foreign language in another country and create a continuous communication in English among students. Develop a joint pen pal project.

● **FIGURE 4.5**

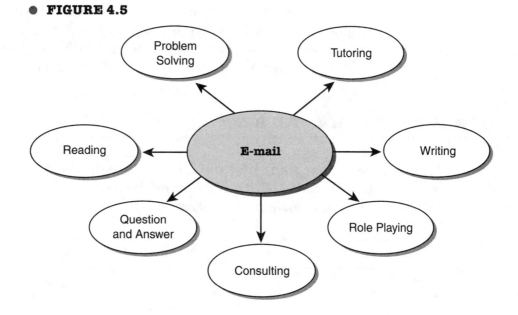

● WHAT'S THE PLAN?

As you develop a lesson plan, think how you can use e-mail for creating a learning community and for more effective student work. (*Hint:* *Think about making your students work in teams in a cooperative model when doing out-of-class assignments.*)

_____

_____

_____

_____

_____

WEB BROWSER

More and more information can be found on the Internet. It has become easier to search for information on the Internet using Web browsers (Google, Yahoo, Netscape Navigator, Mozilla Firefox, Apple Safari, and the like) than to use the traditional library. Any learning activity that needs information can use Web browsing. Students enjoy surfing the Web, so such activities may create a positive attitude toward the assignment. These activities, however, are better used in students' out-of-class work to preserve class time. Students can integrate live links in the texts they write, creating hypertext products.

● WHAT'S THE PLAN?

As you develop a lesson plan, think how you can use browsing the Web for effective student work. (*Hint:* *Think about integrating Web-based resources in student assignments and activities.*)

_____

_____

_____

_____

_____

AUDIO

Audio technology, such as DVD players, iPods, radio, and tape recorders can be used for playing audio text, sounds, and music; a tape recorder can also be used for recording student speech. It is used for developing listening skills, pronunciation, and audio memory; creating sound pictures; and making learning more realistic and effective (Figure 4.6). Suggested activities are:

- Listening to recordings and repeating sounds, words, and sentences helps students to develop listening and pronunciation skills.
- Listening to a song, then learning to sing it (in chorus and individually) helps students to develop pronunciation, vocabulary, grammar, and also cultural appreciation.
- Listening to radio develops students' understanding of oral speech and improves their listening and communication skills.
- Recording their speech and then playing it back develops students' listening, pronunciation, and self-evaluation skills.
- Playing various music in the class during some activities (for example, writing and silent games, especially classical music by Mozart, Haydn, and Handel) has been shown to enhance student learning through positively affecting their emotions (Lozanov & Gateva 1988; Rauscher, Shaw, & Ky 1993; Thompson, Schellenberg, & Husain 2001).
- Playing recordings of various sounds (such as bird singing, wind blowing, running water, traffic in the city, or kitchen work) allows recreation of real-life sounds and thus introduces reality into the classroom, connecting learning to actual experiences, especially when used in appropriate situations.

● **FIGURE 4.6**

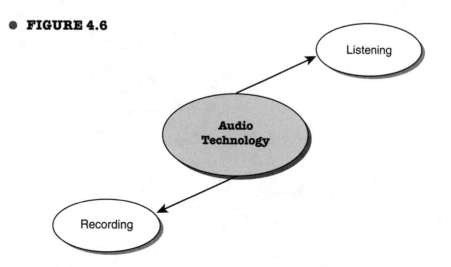

● WHAT'S THE PLAN?

As you develop a lesson plan, think how you can use sounds, audio text, and music for developing student knowledge and skills. (***Hint:*** *Think about integrating the sounds of your students' popular electronic gadgets in their learning.*)

_____

_____

_____

_____

PROJECTION

Projection technology includes devices that help display enlarged pictures on a big screen. Big images produce a stronger impression on the viewers than small pictures in books. Projection devices are made up of overhead projectors that use transparencies, slide projectors that use slides made with a camera, and LCD projectors that project images from the computer. Theatrical movies are also shown with projection devices.

Large pictures are useful to show images of small or detailed objects, tables, charts, and figures. Projection may be effective when explaining new material that needs a higher resolution. Such enlarged pictures can also be used in discussions, role playing, or problem solving, demonstrating an image of an object or situation (Figure 4.7).

● FIGURE 4.7

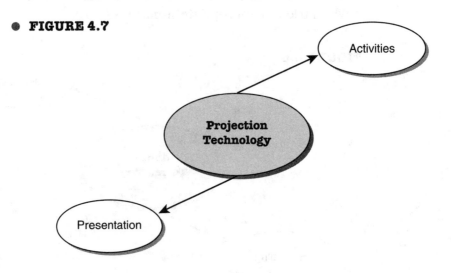

● WHAT'S THE PLAN?

As you develop a lesson plan, think how you can use projection technology to better explain the content. (**Hint:** *Think about using simple ways of demonstrating large images.*)

_____

_____

_____

_____

ET applications should not be limited only to the delivery or presentation of information or to the development of certain skills. In fact, they can greatly affect the emotional state and cognitive processes of the learner. Thus, colored interactive images and video clips seem to catch our attention far better than a plain text. After all, there is a reason for the dramatic popularity of videos and video games. A judicious mix of visual and textual information might well serve the developmental needs of those with various learning styles.

Handouts, Realia, and Manipulatives

The term **handouts** usually refers to material given to students that can extend or enhance the curriculum. A handout can simply contain information (a printed text, a map of California, or the lyrics to "O, Susanna"). Likewise, a handout may, as in the workbook section of this text, give the student an opportunity to "fill in the blanks."

Whether handouts are simply information, require work to be done, or are a combination of both, there is one prerequisite to adhere to: Handouts must not lead to mere information but to meaning. They can fill the learning with meaningful content.

Realia are various real-life objects that help make learning more realistic. They may include price lists from stores that can be used in mathematics class, menus from restaurants in an ESL lesson on how to order a meal, a collection of stones in a science lesson in geology, or chemical substances for chemistry experiments.

Manipulatives are items to aid the learning process. For example, they may be objects used to build structures, as with blocks; to test recollection, as with flash cards; or to count up tangible sums, as with beans.

● WHAT'S THE PLAN?

As you develop a lesson plan, think about the tools you have at your disposal in the classroom that can better develop student knowledge and skills and let you focus more on creative activities, leaving the tedious work to technology. (**Hint:** *Think about using instructional tools, including ET, when this technique can do a better job and save time.*)

_____

_____

_____

_____

Designing an Elementary Classroom

The first thing in setting up an environment where learners can become actively engaged is to organize tables and chairs strategically to allow for flexible grouping. To learn by doing, the physical environment must be set up for social interaction. The key idea is to match structure and function. Because most classrooms are multipurpose, different seating arrangements in different parts of the room should offer your students different learning options. Although a part of your room could be set up for independent study, students need seating arrangements that enhance group activities.

> *The great aim of education is not knowledge but action.*
> (Herbert Spencer, 1820–1903)

Support for the notion that social interaction creates a learning environment is found in the writings of educational psychologists from Vygotsky to Slavin, who have indicated that learning takes place within a social context that engenders meaningful interaction. Let's consider Vygotsky's notion of a zone of proximal development. This zone is premised on what a learner can do alone and what that same learner can do only with others. When setting up a classroom a seating arrangement should optimize sight lines (for example, sitting in a circle) for a focused instructional conversation where learners discuss important ideas, stemming from their personal experiences, while making explicit connections back to the text. These kinds of discussions clearly are facilitated by a single round table and are in concert with Vygotsky's notion that language is a primary vehicle for communicating ideas and enhancing intellectual development (Figure 4.8).

Although focused group conversations are an essential part of the daily activities in your classroom, other physical learning environments must be created to best serve all the different tasks students must perform. Such spatial planning can accommodate special education students, ELL students studying ESL, like-readiness learners, mixed-readiness groups, learners of similar interests, learners of different interests, and peer tutors who act as role models.

● **FIGURE 4.8**

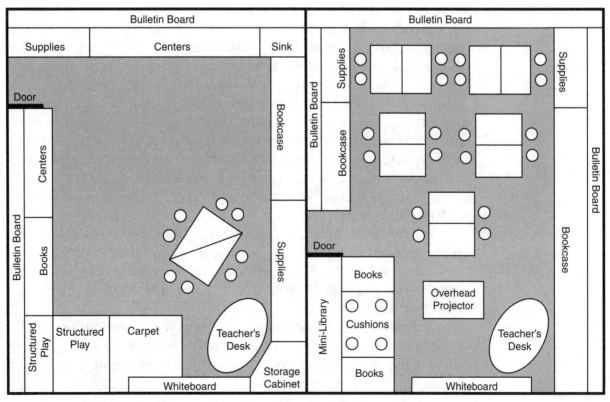

Elementary

Even in a traditional rectangular classroom, you can create many better innovative learning spaces by using shelving and lightweight partitioning to transform various spaces into resource areas. Creative room arrangements allow students to experience learning in a multiplicity of contexts and can enhance performance in an array of developmental tasks.

A key outcome of a multipurpose elementary classroom design is that, as students work in this environment, they develop a sense of "site know-how." Understanding where to go in the room to have different kinds of learning experiences and knowing how to interact with a wide variety of students make for a learning environment that bolsters both academic development and social growth.

Designing a Secondary Classroom

Compared to elementary school, the secondary school has a distinct format where disciplines are divided into different classrooms. For example, when the classroom is constructed for learning science at the secondary level, the focus is not on merely reading or learning about, for instance, chemistry, but on a more hands-on approach—doing chemistry. With an emphasis on experimentation, time (as in extended lab periods) and space (such as worktables) are built in for the collection, discussion, and analysis of data. An adequately designed science classroom should set an atmosphere where small and large groups of students can meet to inquire, plan, conduct investigations, and think critically, constructing both explanations and scientific arguments.

Interactive classrooms positively affect focused communication. A structurally interactive classroom is a model where seating arrangements promote scholarly discourse and expose students to a variety of academic and societal concerns.

Simply put, structure enhances function. Clearly a classroom set up for science (with an equipped lab), for journalism (with access to computers and phones), or for drama (with a stage) are secondary school physical environments that enhance the learning of specific disciplines (Figure 4.9).

In either elementary or secondary classrooms, both group and individual workspaces are provided to meet the needs of students with different learning styles who may be at different stages of academic and/or social development. In short, the physical environment can have a significant impact on learning.

Thus, the way you teach a class is clearly affected by the seating arrangement you use. For example, a cooperative approach needs to have a flexible seating model—seating clusters to implement strategies for organizing group learning activities across and within grade levels. The use of space also has an effect on the efficient use of time. Different activities, with students learning different things at the same time, can take place in the same classroom if proper space provisions are made. For instance, some students can read silently wearing headphones to block out sound while others can view a DVD of Shakespeare's *Henry V* in stereo.

Given your thoughtful classroom design, students have an optimal environment in which to demonstrate their skills and knowledge at the highest level of competence and efficiency. Remember to set up your "model" classroom to reflect the kinds of learning options and alternatives you wish to present to the students.

● **FIGURE 4.9**

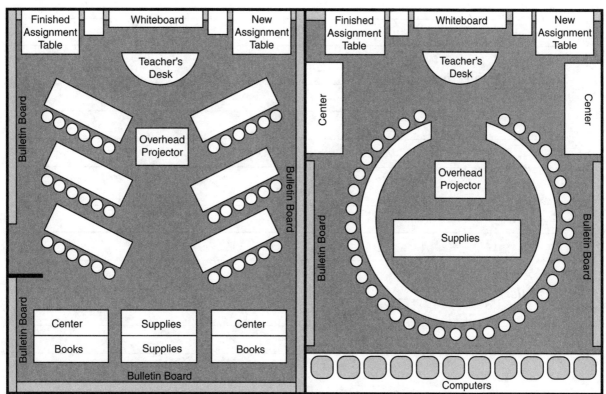

High School

Other important additions to the classroom are instructional tools and materials used to create a real-life environment using visuals (demonstrating slides or video clips when teaching about the environment, transport, travel, culture, shops, and restaurants), realia, and manipulatives (actual objects used in teaching, such as price lists from stores, menus from restaurants, fashion magazines, toy telephones, dishes, and furniture). For instance, when in an ESL or French lesson you teach students to order food at a restaurant in the target language, you can show slides with the restaurant or a video clip at the restaurant or give students menus and invite them to order food in the role-play where one of the students is a patron while another is a waiter.

Your Turn: Practice Sheets

I. MATERIALS AND TOOLS

Topic: _____

_____

Goal and Objectives: _____

_____

_____

_____

Texts: _____

_____

_____

Visuals: _____

_____

_____

Technologies: _____

_____

_____

Handouts, Realia and Manipulatives: _____

_____

_____

II. MATERIALS AND TOOLS

Topic: _____

_____

Goal and Objectives: _____

_____

_____

_____

Texts: _____

_____

_____

Visuals: _____

_____

_____

Technologies: _____

_____

_____

Handouts, Realia and Manipulatives: _____

_____

_____

III. MATERIALS AND TOOLS

Topic: _____

_____

Goal and Objectives: _____

_____

_____

_____

Texts: _____

_____

_____

Visuals: _____

_____

_____

Technologies: _____

_____

_____

Handouts, Realia and Manipulatives: _____

_____

_____

IV. MATERIALS AND TOOLS

Topic: _____

_____

Goal and Objectives: _____

_____

_____

_____

Texts: _____

_____

_____

Visuals: _____

_____

_____

Technologies: _____

_____

_____

Handouts, Realia and Manipulatives: _____

_____

_____

V. MATERIALS AND TOOLS

Topic: _____

_____

Goal and Objectives: _____

_____

_____

_____

Texts: _____

_____

_____

Visuals: _____

_____

_____

Technologies: _____

_____

_____

Handouts, Realia and Manipulatives: _____

_____

_____

> *With so many resource options and alternatives in our basket, it is time now to move to understand the types of procedures to be used in the lesson plan. How we learn to a great extent determines what we learn. Accordingly, what procedures we follow as teachers can open or close the gateway to knowledge for many of our students. Chapter 5 will demonstrate effective procedures you can use in your classroom and beyond.*

CHAPTER 5

....

Procedure

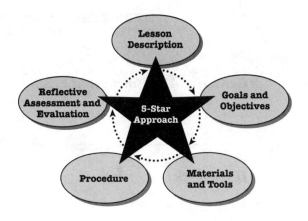

Like a music conductor, the teacher must lead an orchestra according to a set plan. There are strategies and various ways to present a lesson plan, but it is the teacher who must decide on how new material is to be presented and implemented so that every student participates in an active learning environment.

Overview of Procedure
....

Introduction (_____ min.): _____

_____

_____

Homework Checkup (_____ min.): _____

_____

_____

Teacher Presentation (_____ min.): The teacher will:

_____

_____

Class Activities (_____ min.): Students will:

_____

_____

Reflective Assessment and Evaluation (_____ min.): _____

_____

_____

Homework (_____ min.): _____

_____

_____

Closure (_____ min.): The teacher will sum up the lesson naming the major points discussed.

_____

_____

Coming to Terms over Procedure

The 5-Star Lesson Plan consists of five major components: lesson description, goals and objectives, materials and tools, procedure, and reflective assessment and evaluation. While lesson description contains general information about the lesson, such as lesson topic, grade, class characteristics (how many students, how many special education and ELL students, and the like), and standards, a critical part of any lesson is the **procedure** where the teacher and students interact and communicate, share information, solve problems and do assignments to achieve the lesson goals and objectives. It is through procedures that knowledge is constructed and retained and skills are developed and applied.

Lesson procedure is the function of the lesson plan. When implemented in the classroom, the procedure usually runs in five major activities: introduction, new material presentation, activities, assessment/ evaluation, and closure. So we have a 5-Star Lesson Plan implemented in five steps. A crucial factor of effective lesson planning that affects its implementation is the timing of all these steps; the question is how long you and your students should be engaged in a particular activity. Timing, like mortar, holds the lesson structure together. You will allocate time based on lesson goal and objectives, volume of new knowledge, your experience, and class variables. It is convenient to write the time near each activity in minutes, for example, "a collaborative activity—10 minutes" (Figure 5.1).

● **FIGURE 5.1**

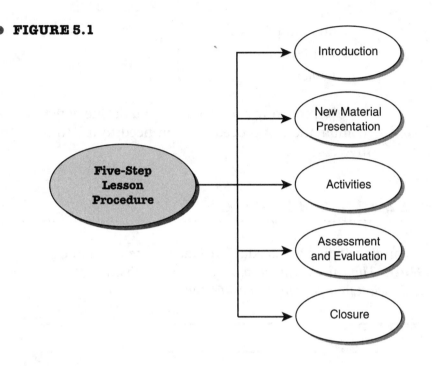

Types of Procedures

There are various types of procedures, and their application is determined by the goals of a particular lesson. Lesson plan development, of course, depends on the types of procedures used. While procedures can been defined conceptually, they almost always are implemented in combination. Here are various types of procedures which are typically found mixed and matched as a lesson plan dictates (Figure 5.2):

1. New content presentation
2. Student activities

● **FIGURE 5.2**

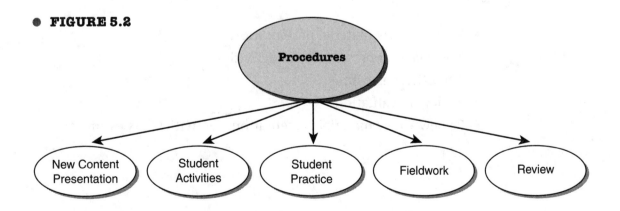

3. Student practice

4. Field work

5. Review

In preparing a lesson plan, you decide which of the procedures or combination of procedures you need to use to meet the lesson objectives.

● WHAT'S THE PLAN?

As you start developing a procedure, decide how you might carry it out. (**Hint:** *Think of the various procedures or combination of procedures you should select from to achieve the objectives.*)

_____

_____

_____

_____

_____

_____

_____

A lesson may be wholly devoted to one type of procedure; however, more often a practical lesson is a combination of several types of procedures. The choice depends on the lesson goals, objectives, lesson content and plan, environment, and students' characteristics (such as responsiveness to today's class needs). Some typical procedural combinations are (Figure 5.3):

- Review + new material presentation
- New material presentation + activities
- Activities + assessment
- Review + evaluation
- Review + new material presentation + activities + assessment

● **FIGURE 5.3**

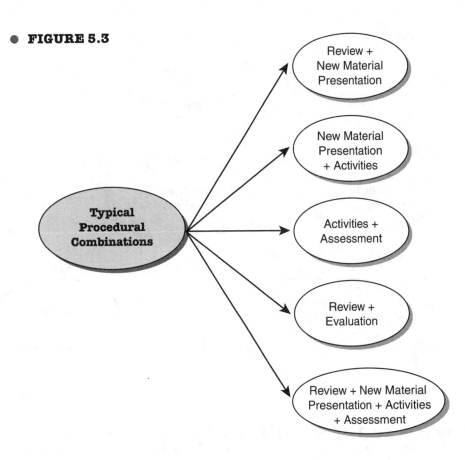

New Material Presentation Module and Its Implementation

New content presentation speaks for itself—it is actually an introduction of the new material. New material presentation may include the following basic activities (Figure 5.4):

- Question-and-answer session (it has two variations: teacher posing a question and then answering it, or teacher asking students to answer and then commenting)
- Teacher lecture and/or demonstration
- Student presentation(s) based on previously given assignment
- Class or independent reading of the text
- Technology-based presentation (e.g. using PowerPoint, video, or multimedia) together with the teacher's lecture or commentaries, or without the teacher's direct participation (e.g. showing a movie)

● **FIGURE 5.4**

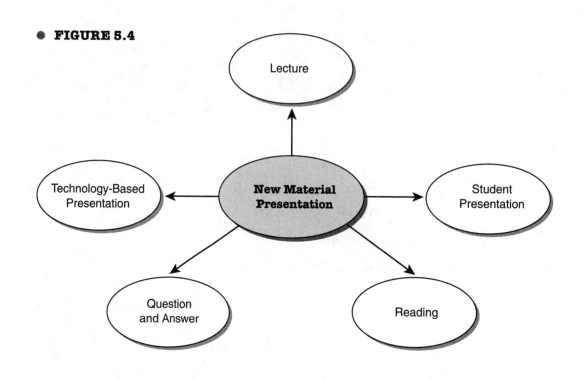

● WHAT'S THE PLAN?

To prepare a presentation of the new material, you should decide what content to present and how you are going to communicate. (***Hint:*** *Think of the various presentation activities you might select from for the content to be effectively acquired, understood, and retained by your students.*)

_____

_____

_____

_____

_____

_____

_____

_____

Homework Checking Module and Its Implementation

To check students' homework is important not only to regulate student preparation for the class but also to reinforce the material for better retention and validate the students' independent work. Homework checkup can include such activities as (Figure 5.5):

- Question-and-answer session
- Quiz on homework
- Written work submission
- Students' oral presentation
- Group project presentation

● **FIGURE 5.5**

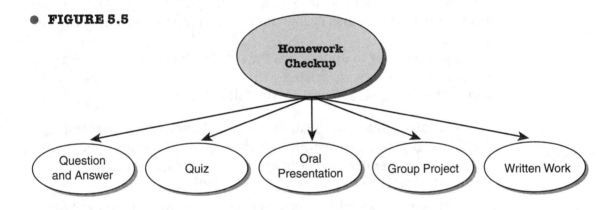

● **W H A T ' S   T H E   P L A N ?**

To review students' homework, decide what activities you are going to use. (**Hint:** *Think of the various activities you should select for student work to be effectively presented, validated, and retained.*)

_____

_____

_____

_____

_____

Coming to Terms over Strategies and Activities

Strategies are particular implementations of a method through specially organized instructional activities. There are strategies for teachers and students. Teacher strategies involve presenting carefully chosen instructional materials, organizing student collaborative and independent work, and managing the class. Student strategies are intended for learners to construct knowledge and develop skills. Student strategies can be for classroom and out-of-classroom use, as in homework, field activities, and community service.

Each strategy is used for a specific purpose. An instructional strategy has a practical goal that should be meaningful to a student. Goals that emanate from a strategy connect learning with real life. On the other hand, an objective states a specific instructional aim of an activity that is to be evaluated. While goals are general in scope, objectives are specific and quantifiable. Measuring the latter allows you to establish whether the goal has been achieved through evaluation at the end of the lesson.

It is important to understand the implicit hierarchy of certain pedagogical terms to best understand where strategies fit in the overall design of the lesson plan. Consider the following:

- A **method** is a theoretical instructional approach. For example, one can practice the communicative approach, accelerated learning, or cooperative learning approaches. All are considered methodological in nature.

- A **strategy,** as we have seen, is a particular implementation of a method through a specially organized instructional activity. For example, reading strategies include, among others, oral reading and sustained silent reading. A student might employ the notion of an outline as a writing strategy to prepare for an essay or a project. Skillful use of an outline can make the final product, the paper itself, a reflection of a clear, concise, and coherent message.

- An **activity** implements a strategy. A strategy in action is an activity. For instance, listening, speaking, reading, writing, dancing, and singing can all be activities that forward a given conceptual strategy. Reciting a poem, writing an outline of a story, solving a problem, or engaging in a dialogue on a topic are examples of activities.

- An **instructional tool** is anything that facilitates teaching and learning. We know that forks or chopsticks are tools for eating. A book, a handout with a text, a felt-tip marker, a transparency, a computer, and software program are all examples of instructional tools.

With these definitions in mind, we can make statements about specific goals and objectives for strategies that relate to fundamental descriptions of lesson plan goals and objectives (see Chapter 3).

Example of a strategy goal: We need to understand the effects of global warming.

Example of strategy objectives: Students will better understand the effects of global warming as they:

- Search, select, evaluate, and process new information
- Disseminate new information in written reports
- Identify five effects of global warming cited in scientific literature
- Take part in a class roundtable to discuss their findings and come up with a proposed set of solutions

● WHAT'S THE PLAN?

Select five best strategies for a particular objective:

_____

_____

_____

_____

_____

Example of strategy goal: Students will be able to conduct a limited dialogue on food preparation and consumption.

Example of strategy objectives: Students will learn and use the new vocabulary while preparing a delicious salad as they:

- Say, spell, and read the words *lettuce, walnuts, raisins, vinegar, olive oil, salad bowl, forks,* and *paper plates*
- Prepare a Greek salad
- Consume the salad
- Take part in a short student-to-student dialog about the experience

(This can be used by both ELL and English-speaking students.)

● WHAT'S THE PLAN?

Construct a set of five strategies and select two which you believe
could be the most effective.

_____

_____

_____

_____

Strategies are seldom used in isolation; usually it takes more than one methodological approach to ensure understanding of new material, concept formation, retention, and automated skill development. For instance, it has been established that it takes multiple uses (dozens of times) of a new foreign word in various contexts (listening, saying aloud, reading, writing, using in speech) to assure its retention and flexible utilization in communication. Therefore, in a lesson for a particular topic or theme, a concise set of strategies and appropriate activities is typically developed. Teachers should base this set on the affective and cognitive needs of their students. It can follow the iterative instructional model, which will be described in this chapter.

An Example: A topic based on textual information to be presented in the class may require four activities (Figure 5.6).

● FIGURE 5.6

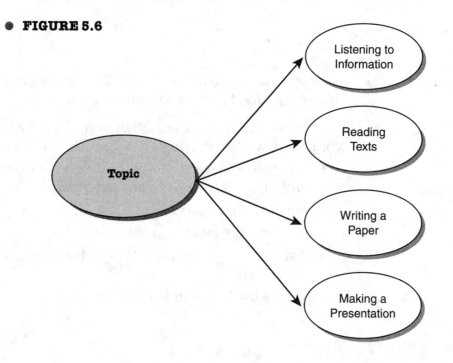

We know a strategy is the particular implementation of a method that operates through specially organized instructional activities. Let's look at these nine component parts that offer an effective structure you can use in your classroom. As you review the list, think of specific examples of each component to make your strategic decisions effective. An instructionally effective strategy usually has the following nine components:

1. Goal
2. Objectives
3. Learning materials necessary to achieve the goal and objectives within a given task, topic, or content
4. A role an individual student will play in this activity
5. Group role characteristics for each participant of the activity, when it is a collaborative one
6. Genuine student motivation to effectively accomplish the activity
7. An appropriate physical or virtual environment that makes up the situation for the activity (simulating real-life circumstances)
8. An outline of the procedure for achieving the planned outcomes (plan of action)
9. Time for implementation

Let's think in terms of a strategy. Imagine you have just been named the coach of the football team. You are excited at the opportunity but at the same time realize that to be a successful coach you must employ a *strategy* by putting into practice a method that you will carry out in your specially organized activities on the practice field. Your *goal* is to win football games. Your *objectives* are to teach the fundamentals so your players will learn and refine various psychomotor activities: how to block, tackle, run with the ball, throw the ball, and catch the ball. You devise *learning materials* that make up your playbook comprised of set plays to achieve your goals by means of successfully demonstrating the objectives. *Individual student roles* are based on your selection, taking into consideration where students feel they can contribute at the various positions (that is, you need to designate linemen, linebackers, backs, and kickers). *Group role characteristics* are critical because, for the team to function at its best, the needs of the team trump individual wants. *Genuine student motivation* is present when the coach sets an environment where members of the team choose to do their best on the field of play. Recall that in football as in life, it is the affective domain (values and emotions) that triggers the cognitive domain (thought) and spurs psychomotor activity (physical action). The *appropriate physical or virtual environment* takes place on the gridiron or the classroom to study video clips of the team's practice or your opponents' games. Your *outline of the procedure for achieving planned outcomes* is inserted into your game plan. Finally, the *time for implementation* is game day! In the next 60 minutes you and your team will face the ultimate evaluation—the scoreboard. As the season proceeds, you will have time for reflective assessment to continually work to improve your team's performance based on the various strategies you employ.

● WHAT'S THE PLAN?

Write your two favorite strategies for second language development.
Identify nine components for each strategy.

_____

_____

_____

_____

_____

Student learning is the raison d'être for teaching. Learner-centered approaches require that teachers facilitate student learning by setting an environment where the main focus in the lesson plan is in promoting student engagement. While the goals and objectives for the student and the teacher may well differ, successful outcomes for the learner remain paramount. For example, students might be geared to practical and realistic endeavors to solve a problem and complete a task. On the other hand, teachers are attempting to set up a lesson plan where students master the new material and develop specific skills. Accordingly, it is the student who plays an active part in most of the activities—not the teacher. Novice teachers tend to lecture and explain ideas and skills resulting in a passive learning experience for the student. However, with a well-constructed lesson plan, active student engagement in learning is promoted due to a superior learning design where the learner chooses to more fully participate in his or her own educational experience. Therefore, students should be given assignments, materials, and *time* to do the job themselves and stay effectively engaged. That is why a lesson plan has to contain a sufficient number of student activities to ensure knowledge construction and development of planned skills while the teacher's work is to create the most enriching and stress-free environment for student learning activities.

There are different ways to classify strategies: by content area, by grade, or by activities, (including teacher or student activities; classroom or out-of-class activities; individual or group activities; reading, writing, communication, and problem-solving activities; role playing; and discussion). We offer a model based on the 5-Star Lesson Plan structure: introduction, presentation, student activities (basic and advanced), closure, homework/extension, and community-based activities.

● WHAT'S THE PLAN?

Write your five favorite strategies for math skill development:

_____

_____

_____

_____

_____

Activities

This section includes a short list of major activities that can be used in you lesson plans.

INTRODUCTION ACTIVITIES

1. Teacher reviewing previous topic
2. Teacher asking questions on the previously learned material
3. Having a student or two review the previous topic
4. Having a few students ask questions on major issues of the previous material and others respond
5. Demonstrating some visuals related to the previous topic and asking students to elaborate
6. Running a short informal review (preferably oral) with questions on the previous topic and then discussing it with the class

NEW MATERIAL PRESENTATION

1. Teacher giving a lecture or a demonstration (accompanied by visuals, video clips, or a PowerPoint presentation) and engaging students in the discussion by asking questions at certain points
2. Selected students making prepared presentation on the new topic
3. Having a guest teacher or presenter speak on a new topic
4. Demonstrating a video (educational movie) or multimedia presentation and commenting
5. Having students search for new information in the texts, online, or in real-life situations (before or during the lesson) and present it to the class

STUDENT ACTIVITIES

Individual

1. Reading a text for meaning
2. Searching for information in printed or electronic sources
3. Observing an object or process (watching a demonstration, an experiment, a real-life situation, or a video clip)
4. Interviewing
5. Constructing or producing an object from parts (Lego, clay figure, maze)
6. Writing a paper (essay)
7. Drawing a picture or a chart
8. Listening (to somebody or to a radio or a recording)
9. Solving a problem
10. Calculating
11. Designing
12. Planning
13. Mimicking or posing (pantomime)
14. Playing a game
15. Presenting or demonstrating
16. Doing physical work or exercise
17. Memorizing
18. Singing
19. Reciting
20. Preparing to participate in a dialogue, a group discussion, or a presentation (including brainstorming)
21. Making a speech

Group (Teamwork, Collaboration, or Cooperation)

Pair Work, Small Group (three to four students),
Large Group (five or more)

1. Discussing
2. Exchanging information
3. Developing a project
4. Performing a joint activity
5. Solving a problem
6. Playing a game
7. Role playing
8. Dramatizing
9. Competing
10. Brainstorming
11. Singing
12. Presenting to a group with a subsequent discussion
13. Going on an excursion or a tour
14. Participating in a community project

Depending on the size of the group, the dynamics of each of these activities will change.

Various Strategies

READING

1. Use the text to find information about . . . and present your findings.
2. Write a short summary of the text.
3. Write a plan of the text.
4. Answer questions on the text.
5. Prepare an essay describing a particular issue discussed in the text.
6. Use the text to write the continuation of the story.
7. Compare issues covered in two texts.
8. Describe a character or a situation.
9. Analyze and critically assess a particular situation in the text.
10. Offer your opinion on the situation described in the text.
11. Prepare to discuss the meaning of the text.
12. Write a critical analysis of the text.

INFORMATION SEARCH

1. Find information on a particular topic.
2. Collect information on a particular topic from three different sources; compare and assess information from all three sources.
3. Describe various ways of gathering information and offer your suggestions for the most efficient collection techniques.

OBSERVATION

1. Look at the picture; what do you want to say about it?
2. Observe the birds in the sky and describe their behavior.
3. Watch a carpenter's (gardener's) work and write an essay about it.
4. Watch a news program: What is the major news of today?

● WHAT'S THE PLAN?

Write your five favorite strategies for reading development.

_____

_____

_____

_____

_____

CONSTRUCTION

1. Make an automobile from Lego parts and describe the process and the outcome.
2. Build a model house and explain how you did it.
3. Assemble words from letter blocks.

WRITING

1. Write a letter to your parents about your trip to the zoo.
2. Write a letter to your friend about your new toys or a book.
3. Write a diary about your summer vacation.
4. Write a story about your friend's adventure.
5. Interview your grandparents about a major event in their life and write a report.

DRAWING

1. Draw a floor plan of your house.
2. Draw a picture based on your favorite story (fairy tale).
3. Draw your toys.

LISTENING

1. Listen to a prerecorded text and repeat words imitating the sounds after the speaker.
2. Listen to a story on tape or DVD and tell the class about it.
3. Listen to a radio broadcast and write a short report.

SOLVING LIFE'S PROBLEMS

1. Here is a problem we have in school . . . offer your solution.
2. You want to buy a new computer game. It costs $80. You have only $55. What are you going to do?
3. Your parents do not allow you to visit your friend's house. Try to convince them to permit the visit.

CALCULATING

1. Calculate how much your family spends on food per month.
2. If you want to walk from your home to school, how long will it take you to get there? (***Hint:*** *Divide the distance by your speed*)

● WHAT'S THE PLAN?

Write your five favorite strategies for writing development:

_____

_____

_____

_____

_____

CLOSURE

1. Teacher reviewing the lesson's main points
2. Students reviewing the lesson's main points
3. Teacher asking questions on the new material

These lists are starting points for activities you can expand to best meet the needs of all of your students.

Activities and Practice

Lesson procedure is focused on developing student understanding of the material, building new knowledge, creating concepts, developing appropriate skills, and constructing personal meaning. The activities selected for the procedure reflect your methodological approach, which, to be most effective, should be geared to your students' learning styles.

Apply learner-centered approaches; reality-based, situated learning; problem solving; case studies; role playing; service learning; team or small-group work and other collaborative activities. Use your students' prior knowledge, which may be found in their authentic personal experiences.

Procedure includes both teacher instructional activities and student learning activities. The former embraces the presentation strategies described above, setting tasks and assignments, prompting students' participation and engagement, facilitating implementation of the learning tasks, using various motivational factors, and supporting student learning. The latter activities may be of at least two levels of complexity: basic activities (guided learning events) and advanced activities (independent practice).

The difference between these levels is that basic activities are to be accomplished according to selected patterns or simple models, with little flexibility in their implementation and under the direction of the teacher. This is done because the objective here is to build primary knowledge and develop initial skills, following a certain sample and using particular limited information. First-level activities include question-and-answer, reading, mnemonic exercises and drills, peer collaboration based on imitation, problem solving, role playing, and educational games (Figure 5.7).

● **FIGURE 5.7**

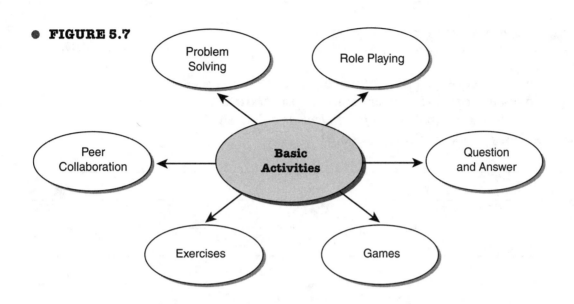

Advanced activities defined as independent practice represent application of the recently learned material and skills in new situations, for example, in a case study or lab experiment. So, independent practice activities can comprise case studies, group work, workshops, independent studies, brainstorming, simulations, research, project development, and student group presentations. (Figure 5.8).

● **FIGURE 5.8**

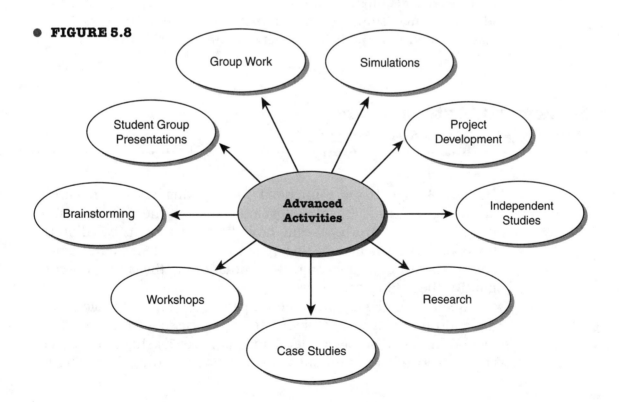

● WHAT'S THE PLAN?

To help students construct new knowledge and develop new skills, decide on what procedures you are going to use. (**Hint:** *Think of the various procedures you should select for students to effectively understand, retain, and use new material and new skills*)

_____

_____

_____

_____

_____

Fieldwork

Fieldwork occurs when students are placed in real-life situations (such as a visit to a zoo or a factory or work in the community) where new knowledge is acquired, manifested, or applied. This activity can be validated through students' presentations and demonstrations in the class, communicating their experiences gained outside the class.

Homework/Extension and Community-Based Activities

Homework activities are intended for ensuring student retention, knowledge construction, skill development, and independent thinking. They cannot just be reading or writing assignments based on the textbook but must be activities requiring the student's autonomous and creative work focused on real-life situations in the family, the community, the nation, and the world.

Some examples are interviewing people on different topics, creating and running a survey, observing and discussing various environmental and social problems, developing projects, making some objects, and participating in community activities and reporting them. This list of activities can certainly be extended. Selection of activities in the lesson planning stage, their organization in the lesson, and their implementation depend on selected strategies that are set to meet the lesson goals and objectives. That teacher develops a strategy focusing on specific goals and objectives that allow students to achieve successful learning outcomes embedded in the lesson plan. A teacher then sets an environment based on an enriched curriculum and a wide variety of methodological approaches and strategies so that students choose to be motivated, engaged, and ultimately empowered.

● WHAT'S THE PLAN?

How would you present the same content in five different ways?
(**Hint:** *Use different modalities, such as lecturing, reading a text, listening to a recording, or viewing a PowerPoint presentation or a video clip*):

_____

_____

_____

_____

_____

_____

An Iterative Instructional Model

Let's discuss two models of the learning process, the linear (sequential) model and the iterative (spiral). Ordinarily, the lesson structure is linear, that is, developing from one step to another (Figure 5.9):

A generic lesson plan model is an example of a linear structure. All the activities in the lesson follow one another. Yet in real learning we usually need to address the same content and skills more than once.

Instruction generally starts with an elementary acknowledgment of the fact that repeated practice is a universal method of learning. *Repetitio est mater studiorum*, says the old Latin proverb. Repetition inherently includes several learning cycles, reiterating or reusing the same content or the same set of instructional activities (Greiner, Serdyukov,

● **FIGURE 5.9**

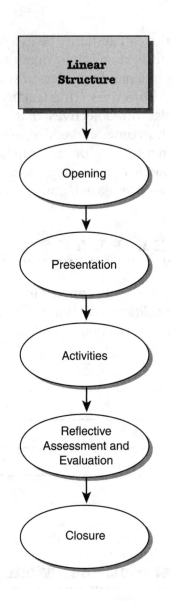

et al. 2005). For example, to master spelling, one repeats the letters of the word *neighbor,* n-e-i-g-h-b-o-r, several times to "embed" the knowledge. One can then assess himself or herself by closing one's eyes so not to look at the spelling word and then repeating the letters in the correct order.

There are also repetitive, cyclic activities in some stages of a lesson (Figure 5.10). For instance, in the presentation phase a teacher can make a short lecture (Presentation 1) then demonstrate a video on the same topic (Presentation 2), and then suggest that students independently find additional information on the topic on the Internet or in the

● **FIGURE 5.10**

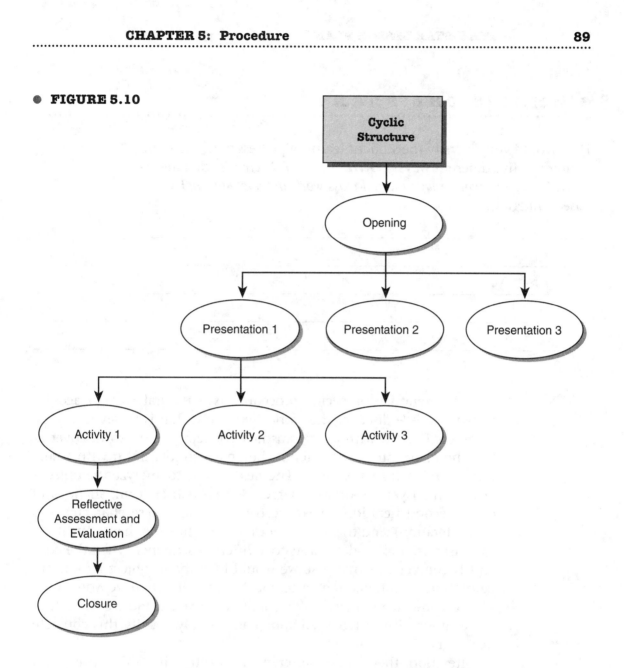

available books (Presentation 3), thus providing a diversified, multi-modal introduction of the new information.

In the activities phase, to ensure better knowledge construction and skill development, various strategies should be applied targeting the same content and same skills. For instance, if students are working on reading, one of the activities (1) can be chorus reading, another (2) could be silent individual reading, and third (3) might be small-group discussion of the items found in the text. This approach guarantees better understanding of information, effective knowledge construction, longer retention, and stronger skills.

● **W H A T ' S   T H E   P L A N ?**

How would you diversify the student learning process with the same content in five different ways? (**Hint:** *Use varied activities that involve individual, pair, small-group, and full-class work and apply technology-based strategies*):

_____

_____

_____

_____

_____

The iterative, or cyclic, procedure is a natural way to acquire knowledge. We discover the world iteratively, that is to say in cycles. Being confronted with a new abstract concept, we try to discover at first the main information about the object to identify it with something familiar (first iteration). The next step is to analyze the object's less essential yet important characteristics, such as form, shape, and color (second iteration). Next we try to classify these characteristics (third iteration), and the process goes on. On the other hand, the iterative instructional model adapts to a different sequence when the concept is concrete. In that case we would identify an object by sensory perceptions (sight, hearing, taste, touch, or smell). Then we would classify the concrete item by thinking about discovering more information (for example, it is a large red apple) and finally classify this concrete item as a fruit.

Iteration, therefore, is different from rote drill in that it is not a mere replication of a previous procedure but a recurrence at a higher level. That is, at each step the cyclic process adds new knowledge to previous knowledge. Thus, iteration as a process presupposes a gradually expanding set of information added to each preceding cycle to increase the initial knowledge and increase learning within each cycle. This process at any point marks an approximation of the current state of the learner as he or she moves to an increased understanding. Reflective assessment and evaluation can be ongoing parts of this dynamic process at any point.

In teaching and learning, this kind of iteration is a repeated procedure carried out during the learning process to provide cyclic levels of increased knowledge presentation, activation, and application. For example, in learning to perform on the piano, the student is presented with the musical score and actively strikes the keys to produce the music. The consistent application of practice can over time produce not only a more refined musical rendition but increase the student's appreciation and, via motor skills, presentation of the piece.

Each cycle contains a model of the whole content area approximated to a given level of knowledge. Each subsequent cycle is based on the preceding one and adds to it some details thus bringing more extended and deeper understanding. Learning starts with the first iteration that presents the whole topic but at first only on an introductory level, without specific details, just major concepts, relationships, and an overall structure. Every subsequent iteration adds new details to the initial presentation, thus increasing its complexity and coverage, until the topic is exhausted. The final iteration is reflective in nature, offering an overview of the topic, recapitulating its principle points.

Therefore, iteration can serve as a mechanism for knowledge construction and management, for improving retention of knowledge, and for effective skill development. The basic idea behind the Iterative Instructional Model is that the learner should learn from previous cycles, expand his or her knowledge, and perform better at every new cycle. Learning actually takes place in a set of iterations. The principle of cycle repetition of activities is used in the Iterative Instructional Model (Greiner, Serdyukov et al. 2005).

The idea of recurrence or repetition is not new. What is different about our approach is the recognition of the organization of the whole learning process as a system of cycles that occur in all stages of the learning process. The cycles be can found at all the levels of the curriculum design, the program, the content area, the unit, and the lesson.

The following are a few examples of the cycles:

Cycle 1. A curricular program contains elements that are interrelated and interdependent; in the beginning of a program students are given its overview.

Cycle 2. Each discipline starts with the introduction previewing its structure, content, activities, and outcomes.

Cycle 3. The specific course is concluded with a reflective general review, highlighting its most essential issues.

Cycle 4. Every lesson begins with the preview of the new plan and ends with the reflective review of the most important items.

These cycles are repetitive in nature.

● WHAT'S THE PLAN?

How can you apply an iterative approach in teaching your content area? (**Hint:** *Think of doing the same activity in five different ways.*)

_____

_____

_____

_____

_____

_____

The interrelations between the learning modules and cycles are not vertical, rather they are built into a spiral, with each lower level connected to and spiraling to the next higher level.

There are several significant implications to the Iterative Instructional Model. The cyclic approach helps to improve the structure and organization of the delivery of curriculum and of the students' learning. It provides a better conceptual understanding of the curricular content because it continuously supports the integral vision of the spiral. A **spiral curriculum** develops, revisiting foundational concepts repeatedly, constructing on them new knowledge as the learner better understands the meaning and depth of what is being studied. This approach also allows demonstrating and applying the links between each topic of a course of study with other topics and with other courses in a program, thus developing interdisciplinary links.

Two or more cycles covering one topic may have a common practicum, student presentations, a video with discussion, a visitor presentation with a subsequent student question-and-answer session or discussion, a story narration, a general discussion, and a text. This model can in many cases provide greater information retention and better skill development than a strictly linear approach.

Another example demonstrates the application of this model in a set of several cyclic activities, each of which is focused on developing communicative ESL skills based on the same content (words and phrases)—see the "Making Acquaintances" set of activities (Chapter 8). We are aware that a communicative skill develops through numerous applications of the same language material in cyclic communicative situations.

There are nine cyclic activities in this set, each similar to all the others in objective, content, and process. The only difference among them is in changing tasks and communicative partners, which provides for a nonmonotonous and, consequently, varied repetitions of the same content in similar acts. Thus, this cyclic set ensures the necessary recurrence of the same activity in different circumstances for developing a sound skill and ensuring better retention of the designated language material without it necessarily becoming tedious.

To review, the overall process of knowledge construction based on the Iterative Instructional Model connects each lower-level activity to higher levels like a spiral. Its goal is gradual accumulation of knowledge in each of the cycles to an ever-fuller representation. Each preceding cycle grows into the subsequent one, expanding the knowledge at each iteration. Each cycle represents a full model of the whole topic presented at a consecutively greater level of complexity, completeness, and detail than the previous one (Figure 5.11).

The Iterative Instructional Model can be applied in the presentation phase where the content is cycled several times in different modalities (lecture, instructor demonstration, text, visuals, audiovisual or multimedia program, and simulations). It is important in this cyclic structure that the topic is presented as a whole, in its entirety, though several increasing levels of presentation. In this way students perceive and process information a number of times in multiple formats, which improves understanding and retention.

The Iterative Instructional Model is particularly useful for effective knowledge construction and sound skill development. In the application phase, where students demonstrate their new knowledge and skills in dealing with various life-based situations, this model helps to integrate new knowledge and skills to real-life situations.

● **FIGURE 5.11**

Spiral
An expanding spiral
(one iteration grows
into the others)

● WHAT'S THE PLAN?

How would you explain the Iterative Instructional Model to your colleagues? (**Hint:** *Think of repetition, life cycles, and other recurrent activities we use.*)

_____

_____

_____

_____

_____

Final Thoughts and Terms

Recall that the differences among school subjects are not only in the content but also in the conceptual flow of the class. Methodologically speaking, a given course (science, math, drama) may call into use different cognitive processes that require distinct activities. The lessons in these classes may have similar structure but differ in content, concepts, and instructional strategies. This means that you may have to develop a specific set of strategies, activities, assignments, assessment tools, and techniques for each discipline you teach.

Below is a framework for your lesson procedure. Please recall what is each component's function.

Introduction: _____

_____

_____

Homework Checkup: _____

_____

_____

Teacher Presentation: The teacher will:

_____

_____

Accommodations for ELL/ SDAIE: _____

_____

_____

Class Activities: Students will:

_____

_____

Reflective Assessment and Evaluation: _____

_____

_____

Homework: _____

_____

Closure: The teacher will sum up the lesson naming the major
points discussed.

_____

_____

To Sum Up

The **introduction** is the initial part or phase of the lesson, intended
to prepare students for learning by warming up, general conversation,
reviewing the previous lesson's key points, setting the objectives, presenting the plan of the current lesson, and doing preliminary exercises.
Here the rationale for the lesson is given, including the state content
standards and the explanation of why the lesson is important for the
learner. Goals and objectives have to be explained to the students so
they know what they will be doing and why. In every lesson, the
teacher should always make reference to what is being learned, why it
is important for the student, and how it relates to other learning.
Therefore, the learner should be aware of the relevance of a specific
skill or a given activity. The general demeanor of a caring and competent teacher is essential at this stage of the lesson to lower the students'
level of anxiety.

Homework checkup to be reviewed in class is a stage during which the students present their assigned out-of-class work, either by making oral presentations or by turning in written work. It is important that the students realize that "we don't do disposable work."

Presentation is the phase where the new material is introduced by the teacher in the form of an expository lecture, a narrative, or by reading from a text. Often the teacher uses various visuals germane to the area of study. Video or multimedia can be very effective presentation tools. Presentation can at times be made by students. This phase is extremely important as it sets the model from which the students will learn.

Classroom activities make up the phase when students perform various assignments, individual or collaborative, among which are problem solving, case studies, discussions, exercises, role playing, games, experimenting, and demonstrating. These activities may be of at least two levels of complexity, basic (guided activities) and advanced (independent practice).

The difference between these levels is as follows: Basic activities are to be accomplished according to patterns or simple models, with little flexibility in their implementation and controlled by the teacher. This is done on purpose because the objective here is to develop initial skills, imitating a certain sample and using particular limited knowledge. In teaching English language learners, you may include various language exercises, such as drills, Cloze testing, substitution, multiple choice, and simple communicative exercises, such as simulation and role playing.

Advanced activities are less controlled (some teacher guidance can be helpful, nonetheless) and allow for more freedom and flexibility in their implementation. Students are not limited in their performance except by the task, setting, and purpose of the particular activity. Examples of practice are dramatization and project presentations. An important aspect of all activities is the application of the new material and skills in real-life situations or simulated practice, whether it is in the classroom, on the computer, in homework, or in field and community activities outside school.

Homework is vital for providing further independent learning and real-life applications and experiences; it is also needed for assuring retention. Home assignments extend classroom learning and as such should include creative, rather than just regurgitating, tasks (for example, collecting information or samples, interviewing or helping people, searching for and processing information for a project, solving a problem or writing an essay).

After the homework has been corrected, and if need be revised, to be brought up to standard, it is posted in the classroom. A classroom full of high-quality student work provides a model for more high quality output. When the class bulletin boards are full, old work is taken down and put in a portfolio for the rest of the term. This honors the work and provides a quantitative and qualitative record for teachers, students, parents, and administrators.

Closure is a phase that incorporates the review of the lesson and the summary of the lesson's key points. It can also include a general appraisal (assessment and evaluation) of the students' work and a short preview of the lesson to come. Closure is important, as it leaves a lasting imprint in students' minds; people usually remember what was said in the beginning and in the end of the conversation.

Last but not least, instructional support includes everything needed for successful teaching and learning during a lesson—for example, teaching and learning materials, visuals (charts, pictures, text on the posters), manipulatives, and realia. Also critical to the contemporary classroom is technology in terms of the hardware and software, which allows for more efficient knowledge presentation and effective learning and presents the teacher the option to make an otherwise traditional synchronous environment asynchronous. The lesson as a procedure takes place in an actual physical environment comprised of a classroom set up to enhance the learning process (for example, the specific placement of desks and chairs for optimal perception of information and effective activities, visuals and instructional materials hung on the walls, and fresh air).

Suitable **accommodation** can help ensure the learning process for every student. The authors use the most encompassing view of the notion of inclusion to cover all students. Some accommodations for ELL students are:

- Allowing extra time when necessary for a student to complete the task
- Understanding the student's learning styles (whether tactile, kinesthetic, visual, or auditory) and making appropriate modifications
- Providing bilingual dictionaries and handout glossaries
- Offering to clarify definitions of words and concepts using culturally based analogies
- Engaging in appropriate-level English grammar and vocabulary to make the curriculum more comprehensible to ELLs without compromising the quality of what is taught
- Integrating peer teaching and collaborative activities including all students
- Using bilingual teacher aids when available
- Having individual consultations after class when necessary

Your Turn: Practice Sheets

Now it is your turn to practice writing out the procedure portion of the lesson plan. Do five examples. Think of the block of time you have to teach a lesson and then approximate how long you will need (in minutes) to complete each of the six steps in the procedure section.

I. PROCEDURE

Introduction (_____ min.): _____

_____

_____

Homework Checkup (_____ min.): _____

_____

_____

Teacher Presentation (_____ min.): The teacher will:

_____

_____

Class Activities (_____ min.): Students will:

_____

_____

Reflective Assessment and Evaluation (_____ min.): _____

_____

_____

Homework (_____ min.): _____

_____

_____

Closure (_____ min.): The teacher will sum up the lesson naming the major points discussed.

_____

_____

II. PROCEDURE

Introduction (_____ min.): _____

_____

_____

Homework Checkup (_____ min.): _____

_____

_____

Teacher Presentation (_____ min.): The teacher will:

_____

_____

Class Activities (_____ min.): Students will:

_____

_____

Reflective Assessment and Evaluation (_____ min.): _____

_____

_____

Homework (_____ min.): _____

_____

_____

Closure (_____ min.): The teacher will sum up the lesson naming the major points discussed.

_____

_____

III. PROCEDURE

Introduction (_____ min.): _____

_____

_____

Homework Checkup (_____ min.): _____

_____

_____

Teacher Presentation (_____ min.): The teacher will:

_____

_____

Class Activities (_____ min.): Students will:

_____

_____

Reflective Assessment and Evaluation (_____ min.): _____

_____

_____

Homework (_____ min.): _____

_____

_____

Closure (_____ min.): The teacher will sum up the lesson naming
the major points discussed.

_____

_____

IV. PROCEDURE

Introduction (_____ min.): _____

_____

_____

Homework Checkup (_____ min.): _____

_____

_____

Teacher Presentation (_____ min.): The teacher will:

_____

_____

Class Activities (_____ min.): Students will:

_____

_____

Reflective Assessment and Evaluation (_____ min.): _____

_____

_____

Homework (_____ min.): _____

_____

_____

Closure (_____ min.): The teacher will sum up the lesson naming
the major points discussed.

_____

_____

V. PROCEDURE

Introduction (_____ min.): _____

_____

_____

Homework Checkup (_____ min.): _____

_____

_____

Teacher Presentation (_____ min.): The teacher will:

_____

_____

Class Activities (_____ min.): Students will:

_____

_____

Reflective Assessment and Evaluation (_____ min.): _____

_____

_____

Homework (_____ min.): _____

_____

_____

Closure (_____ min.): The teacher will sum up the lesson naming the major points discussed.

_____

_____

Moving through the various decisions a teacher makes as to what procedures to follow in a given lesson plan is premised to a great extent on the expected outcomes. How do we know our teaching was effective? The simple answer is because students have learned more that they knew before. The real questions are, how does a teacher assess learning? How does a teacher evaluate learning? Chapter 6 will answer both those questions and point to a critical difference between assessment and evaluation.

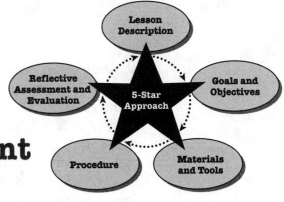

Reflective Assessment and Evaluation

*M*easuring how much a student has learned gives us valuable information about the efficacy of the lesson plan and the instruction. Within the measuring process, an enlightened teacher needs to know the difference between assessment and evaluation, what the characteristics of each measurement tool are—and when best to use them to enhance the learning environment.

Overview of Reflective Assessment and Evaluation

Assessment: _____

_____

_____

Evaluation: _____

_____

_____

Coming to Terms over Assessment and Evaluation

Perhaps one of the most frequently used terms in modern pedagogy is the word *assessment*. Within educational circles, assessment has come to imply a panoply of meanings, including grades, scores, rubrics, criteria, evaluation, performance, and proficiency, plus both formative and summative judgments. In fact, the wide area of multiple meanings encompassed by the word *assessment* has made it, in terms of common usage within the field of education, more and more often interchangeable with the term *evaluation.* Is there a difference? The short and unfortunate answer is no. Assessment and evaluation have become to be used synonymously in the area of educational discourse. However, the longer answer is that there should be a difference, and there is an etymological root for such a clear distinction.

The authors believe the lack of discernable difference between assessment and evaluation in the professional vernacular is most regrettable. It may well be that the lack of distinction between these two words has lead to so-called "assessment" tools (such as the SAT, MSAT, GRE, and the like), which traditionally have acted as evaluations and have had a well-documented history of determining the academic futures of millions of students, based on a norm-referenced ranking system. That these so-called assessment tests are dispositive of who is admitted to higher levels of learning in a sense contradicts the original meaning of the idea of assessment.

In fact, **assessment,** which is inherently reflective, is derived from the Latin *assidere,* which literally means "to sit beside." If one can imagine an examiner sitting alongside a student and providing feedback (based on observing, documenting, and analyzing the learner's work), we can better understand how the student is to accomplish genuine assessment, which is ultimately self-assessment. The assessor provides information; however, it is the assessed who must accept or reject the findings.

● WHAT'S THE PLAN?

How are you going to assess students? (**Hint:** *How would you conduct ongoing informal discussions with students to identify their strengths and weaknesses?*)

_____

_____

_____

_____

_____

Too often the information from an evaluation (such as a standardized test) is seen as conclusive proof, used to separate the wheat from the chaff (as in the case of acceptance to a school), and students simply believe the results of so-called assessment tools that are actually evaluation tools. Assessment requires the critical step of reflective self-assessment. Such a misuse of the concept of assessment (which should aid a learner to know his or her strengths and weaknesses) has provided a basis for schools improperly and unethically to use so-called assessments as exclusionary tools. Giving precise definitions of words commonly used in a pedagogic discussion brings greater clarity in professional discourse and better serves the purpose of assessment and evaluation as distinct areas of judgment.

The authors argue that the concepts of grades, scores, and rankings be stricken from the definition of assessment. Therefore, the emphasis on assessment should be the empowering act of the learner to experience self-review based on the feedback by a qualified examiner. Ultimately, requisite learner reflection brings about new self-knowledge.

In short, **evaluation** is a static event that is represented by a grade, a rank, or a score that is a snapshot of how well a student does on a particular test on a particular day. On the other hand, an **assessment** is a dynamic process that serves as a point of departure to better know oneself. Therefore, assessment is a procedural phenomenon, while evaluation is a finite occurrence.

● WHAT'S THE PLAN?

When is it appropriate to evaluate your students? (**Hint:** *When is formal testing [such as true-and-false, multiple-choice, or essay exams] most appropriate, and what form it might take?*)

_____

_____

_____

_____

_____

To avoid this all-too-common ambiguity, specific attributes to better describe these two terms are presented in Figure 6.1.

● **FIGURE 6.1**

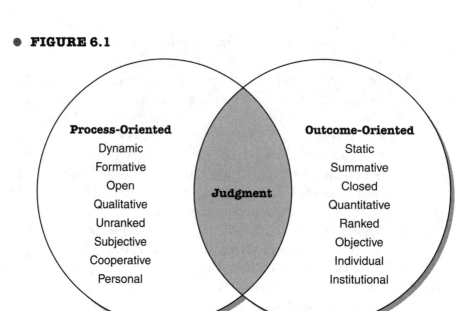

Process-Oriented	Judgment	Outcome-Oriented
Dynamic		Static
Formative		Summative
Open		Closed
Qualitative		Quantitative
Unranked		Ranked
Subjective		Objective
Cooperative		Individual
Personal		Institutional
Assessment		**Evaluation**

Assessment and evaluation form a relationship that is both complimentary and vital to the educational process. Concepts of both instructional time and educational paradigm are quite distinct. Let us first consider how time plays a critical role in the difference between assessment and evaluation. An assessment is fundamentally an evolutionary process of enhancing one's self-knowledge based on the feedback that continuously helps the learner to adapt to different learning environments. It is like the continuously changing image of the movie.

On the other hand, an evaluation is like a freeze-frame of the movie. Recall that evaluation is a one-time glimpse of a student's knowledge expressed in a score, ranking, or grade that exists at a given point in time. Accordingly, the difference between assessment and evaluation is similar to the difference between animation and still life. These two forms of pedagogical judgment reside in different paradigms—one centered on the learner, the other more concerned with the program or a school. In an assessment, one is compared only to himself or herself to better know that self. In an evaluation, one is compared to others primarily to better understand the efficacy of a program or an entire institution.

GRADING

> *Teachers do not give grades, students earn their grades.*

Grading is a judgment of a student's work based on measurement and numerical evaluation. It may become confusing for both students and teachers if different ranking systems are used. The best policy might be a traditional 100-point scale. All assignments are given a certain number of points according to their educational value. The total of all assignments in a term should be equal to 100, which not only makes it easier for you to calculate the final grade but also makes it easier for a student to conceptualize. A score is a point total that is part of a tangible grading criterion. The score is then applied to an accepted scale, which yields a letter grade.

Scoring Scale

100–93 = A

92–85 = B

84–75 = C

74–60 = D

59–0 = F

While it is easy to sum up the points for an objective test (such as a multiple-choice or true-and-false exam), it is more difficult to score a short-answer or an essay test. Fair and accurate evaluation in reflective writing demands that both the teacher and student be aware of published transparent grading criteria.

The element of quality is at its root subjective. The element of quantity, on the other hand, is an objective measure. To eliminate either of these two elements from grading would lead to an inferior conceptual model. Moreover, a universal philosophical law of transformation of quantity into quality states that quality emanates from quantity (Engels 1987). This law can be illustrated via skill development, where the only way for a skill to develop is through sufficient practice.

For grading criteria to function successfully, they must be viewed as dispositive by both the evaluator and the person whose work is being evaluated. Therefore, a judicious mix of both the factors of quality and quantity in a written assignment are outlined in a five-point scale that asks the student to demonstrate higher-order critical thinking skills (such as analysis, synthesis, and evaluation) by means of a written composition:

1. Complexity of ideas (cogent response to specific question)
2. Quality and quantity of detail (for example, explicit connections to course materials)
3. Organization (standard format)
4. Correctness (grammar, syntax)
5. Fluency (determined by amount written)

Grading, unfortunately, can cause anxiety for both the teachers and the student. Let's look at three aspects of grading:

- Grading on the bell curve
- Giving grades versus earning grades
- Helpful hints for grading policies

The bell curve is commonly thought of as a "balanced" curve. This notion is based on the idea that a bell-shaped curve in some way "proves" the reliability of the scores and the validity of a test. In short, a test that results in a few A's and F's, a larger number of D's and B's, and a great majority of C's appears desirable to many. The thought is that because the scale resembles the "perfect" bell curve, such a test must be "fair."

The problem is that these beliefs are unwarranted and even more importantly may do great harm to students. In fact, a perfect normal distribution curve does not inherently have anything to do with fairness—the bell curve is but a theoretical concept.

For an example of how the bell-curve mentality operates against setting and then achieving lofty goals, look at the real world. If you were a surgeon who, year after year, lost as many patients on the operating table as you saved, would you consider your record "perfect" and expect to open a successful private practice? If you were a home builder who turned out as many good homes as defective ones, with many average homes in between, how long do you think this "perfect" distribution would keep you in business?

When you find that a certain segment of the class does not understand the lesson you can either accept the failure as part of a "bell curve" or intervene to reteach and retest. If you wish to give a "fair" chance to all, start by using different approaches to appeal to different learning styles, using more effective strategies and activities, contacting parents to enlist their support when students appear to be falling behind, and adjusting your lesson plan.

Your professional responsibility is to produce lesson plans containing evaluation systems that actively work to bring all students up to standard. Be a committed student advocate. Your success is not premised on the pseudoscientific "perfect" balance of failure and success but on the number of students who have learned.

As a teacher, are you expected to give grades? If you think the answer is yes, think again. Grades should be earned by the students and not given by the teacher.

Think of it this way. Students are the players who score the points, and teachers, in assigning grades, are merely the scorekeepers. As a teacher, you cannot give what you don't have. Grades, after all, are the product of student achievement. Therefore grades are not something "supplied" by the teacher.

Here are some helpful hints to assigning fair grades:

- Grading policy must be fair, straightforward, simple, clear, objective, and understood by the students and their parents.

- A concise handout outlining the grading policy should be distributed by the teacher at the beginning of each term or available on an Internet site.

- Students should have immediate access to their current grades at any given point during the term.

- You should give periodic updates to the parents. This can be accomplished by an Internet site or by phoning parents with progress reports.

Your grading procedures should be "an open book." While you manage the procedure, it is the student who controls his or her academic future by earning good grades.

At the end of a given evaluation, points are summed up to reveal the scores to be translated into the grades each student earns. Accountability is a learned behavior. A student in your classroom needs to understand by way of your personal guidance and grading policy that the responsibility for his or her grade ultimately resides with that student—the person who earned that grade.

Parents know more than children.

Student–Teacher–Parent Conference

An assessment process that includes a student–teacher–parent conference, where the student acts as the presenter, is a wonderful way for the learner to assume greater control over his or her education.

This three-way process or troika model allows the student to become an active participant in an ongoing process of assessment. The teacher's role is that of expert assessor, while the parents' contribution is one of expert personal knowledge about their son or daughter. It should also be noted that parental involvement in this process brings huge value to the conference and facilitates follow-up measures (Figure 6.2).

● **FIGURE 6.2**

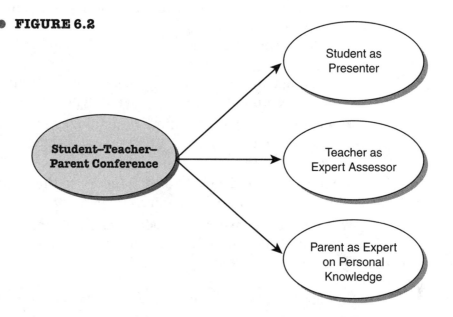

Documentation that might serve as a basis for these conferences includes archived quizzes, tests, homework, essays, audio or video files—in other words, the student's typical work that may be found in his or her portfolio. While sharing the contents of one's portfolio, it is the student as the presenter who explains the *what, how,* and *why* of each artifact (Figure 6.3).

The central idea is to connect in a three-way mutual problem-solving process that highlights student accountability in which the

● **FIGURE 6.3**

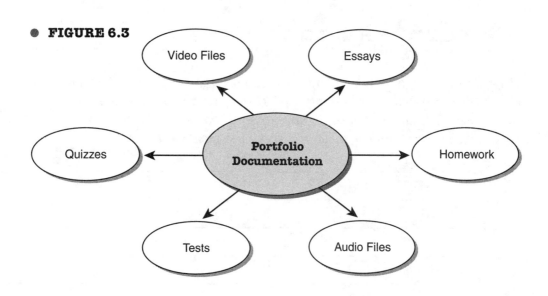

student articulates how he or she, via the evidence supplied, is building small successes into larger ones.

Although there is a clear focus on the student's cognitive development, the affective component of greater self-esteem and personal satisfaction is of immense significance. Students who achieve, and can explain how they achieved, grow in a sense of self-efficacy and are more likely to continue to be successful in future endeavors.

The goals of conferences are to:

- Educate the student-presenter to the process of self-assessment
- Promote acceptance of responsibility on the part of the student-presenter for academic development and social growth
- Enhance the student-presenter's higher-order critical thinking skills to analyze, synthesize, and evaluate on an ongoing basis
- Pursue open and honest communication among all parities and, if need be, revision of student work

This procedure can be carried out in a traditional classroom, over the phone, or even asynchronously over the Internet. What is important is that it is an ongoing process designed to give the student an opportunity to present his or her work and receive valuable feedback.

● WHAT'S THE PLAN?

How would you go about setting up a student–parent–teacher conference? (***Hint:*** *Would you use portfolios? How often would you hold the conferences? Would all conferences have to be held at school? What would you as a teacher recommend to address specific student weaknesses?*)

_____

_____

_____

_____

_____

Learning Assessment and Revision

An important part of learning is a developed ability to self-assess and learn and to be able to critically analyze oneself and one's work. We have to help our students to learn to review, reflect, and improve. Revision, which is a reflective process, is also an integrative procedure that requires refinement of thought. A student who reshapes assigned tasks actually discovers new and hopefully more meaningful ways of perceiving knowledge.

To revise, a student must have acquired a level of communicative skills, understood some information, and conceptualized an alternative course of action. Clearly, revision can enhance reflective thinking and should be viewed by all as a normal and valued way to enhance one's ability to clarify one's ideas.

Revision is clearly a learner-centered process. As a teacher you should set an environment where this activity is not seen as punishment or reprimand but as an opportunity through which the student can choose to be empowered by reengineering better work.

For example, let's consider revising an essay. Clearly, it is the student who must, in the final analysis, reevaluate his or her writing by reflecting on what was written (that is, embedded knowledge), why it was written (the reason behind the work) and how it can be modified (through word choice, grammar, logical connections, and conclusions). For a reflective writer it is not enough to impart information; what is called for is meaning.

● WHAT'S THE PLAN?

How would you present the concept of revision to your students?
(**Hint:** *How can you make revision part of a learning process rather than a perceived chore?*)

_____

_____

_____

_____

_____

Testing

Which tests are best? A short answer might be that the widest variety of testing provides the learner with multiple ways to demonstrate to the teacher what he or she has learned. So, when many types of tests are given, both teachers and learners have various forms of evidence of learner accomplishments.

Using many different kinds of evaluation tools may be the best way to get the most "snapshots" of what a student knows. Nevertheless, let's remember that learning involves critical thinking skills. Recalling that reflective thought is synonymous to higher-order thinking, and an essay exam is clearly more apropos than an objective true-and-false or multiple-choice test.

An essay is a much more demanding examination of critical thinking skills. In a successful essay a student must:

- Introduce an organized coherent answer
- Move from information to meaning
- Discuss logical connections
- Sum up the critical points
- Come to conclusions

A student's writing is one of the most valid tests because a student must integrate various language and higher-order skills to be successful. An effective answer to this kind of test can reflect a depth of knowledge not present in an objective exam (for example, a true-and false-or multiple-choice test).

Authentic Assessment and Evaluation, and Metacognition

Authentic assessment and evaluation occur when a teacher makes a direct examination of the learner's performance on a given task. Authentic assessment and evaluation are more that just the learner's recall of information—they require the student to perform a task that will be judged.

For instance, there is a difference between writing about hitting a 90-mile-an-hour fastball thrown by Roger Clemens and actually doing so! Performance is the key ingredient in authentic assessment and evaluation.

In the classroom, instead of students marking a T or F, or selecting one of four options on a multiple-choice quiz, or making decisions on a traditional test, an authentic appraisal can be seen in a portfolio where a wide range of students' works, such as writings, video clips of activities and performances, records of assignments and discussions, and other artifacts are to be accumulated over the course of study.

Authentic tests have more inherent validity in that they examine responses in a real-world environment. For example, let's consider a piano recital. The pianist must focus his or her comprehensive knowledge on one musical piece with skill and artistic creativity to be successful. A pencil-and-paper test on how to play Bach is at best simplistic and at worst seems a bit silly.

The needs of learners appear best supported by authentic testing that applies to the real world in which they must live after the three o'clock school bell rings. As for the teacher, it seems clear that it is easier to assess a student and also improve teaching methods based on an authentic assessment rather than try to interpret the proxy items of a traditional test, which are indirect indications at best of a skill or of comprehensive knowledge.

There is a link between authentic assessment and evaluation and metacognition. When we think about how we think, we also are assessing how well we do. This process is called metacognition.

As a learner becomes successful in a number of learning situations, there occurs a recognition that certain learning strategies can transfer from one situation to another. For example, the knowledge of and strategy in acquiring basic vocabulary appears to be the same whether one is studying history, math, science—or even a foreign language. Not only are certain learning strategies transferable, but many skills, including language skills, can be transferred. For instance, there never was a good writer who was not first a good reader. Correspondingly, math skills are critical for developing problem-solving skills in sciences like physics and chemistry. In a holistic sense, skills are interdependent. This is a critical notion when building an effective lesson. This point has very important implications regarding the curricular base of lesson plans for a population ever more culturally and linguistically diverse. When we look at bilingual education, for instance, we need to note that language acquisition is a skill-based enterprise. Therefore, in learning to read English it is essential that the learner of English as a foreign or second language knows how to read in his or her native language. One cannot transfer a skill one does not possess.

Awareness of how one thinks is a valuable learning tool. Teachers have a role to play in modeling metacognitive behaviors. To model metacognitive behavior one must be focused on process as well as outcomes.

In short, metacognition is critical to the ultimate goal of education—the emergence of a lifelong self-directed learner—a learner who knows how he or she learns. Such a learner not only knows how he or she learns but is better able to articulate what and why they learn.

● WHAT'S THE PLAN?

How do you decide which kind of test (authentic, true and false, multiple choice) best fits the needs of your lesson plan? (**Hint:** *What kind of knowledge and to what depth are you asking students to demonstrate*)?

_____

_____

_____

_____

_____

Your Turn: Practice Sheets

Write out five different assessment and evaluation segments of classes you are teaching or plan to teach. Reflect on the options and alternatives you have for both assessment and evaluation.

I. REFLECTIVE ASSESSMENT AND EVALUATION

Projected Learning Outcome: _____

_____

_____

Assessment: _____

_____

_____

Evaluation: _____

_____

_____

II. REFLECTIVE ASSESSMENT AND EVALUATION

Projected Learning Outcome: _____

_____

_____

Assessment: _____

_____

_____

Evaluation: _____

_____

_____

III. REFLECTIVE ASSESSMENT AND EVALUATION

Projected Learning Outcome: _____

_____

_____

Assessment: _____

_____

_____

Evaluation: _____

_____

_____

IV. REFLECTIVE ASSESSMENT AND EVALUATION

Projected Learning Outcome: _____

_____

_____

Assessment: _____

_____

_____

Evaluation: _____

_____

_____

V. REFLECTIVE ASSESSMENT AND EVALUATION

Projected Learning Outcome: _____

_____

_____

Assessment: _____

_____

_____

Evaluation: _____

_____

_____

Now that we have looked at measurement and can both assess and evaluate learning, let's reflect and refocus—based on your measurements—on how best to continue to construct knowledge and skill development in the classroom. Chapter 7 will consider the organizing, structuring, and modeling that takes place within your lesson plans. These notions are not to be thought of as static ideas but as dynamic concepts that allow for multiple approaches in planning and implementing a lesson to meet the needs of your students.

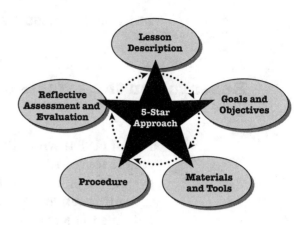

CHAPTER 7

Time Efficiency in Teaching and Learning

We have just seen how reflective assessment and evaluation are about appreciating, measuring, and judging learning. These functions are an inherent part of education. One thing you will constantly measure in the classroom is time. Research on the concept of time demonstrates its critical value as an integral variable in any lesson plan. This chapter will outline the best uses of time from the traditional classroom periods punctuated by school bells to online education where an asynchronous design treats time in a very different manner.

Coming to Terms over Time

Time is a most significant commodity for a teacher and for a learner because it demands modifications in curricular and methodological considerations. These changes affect your lesson plan. Making teaching and learning more efficient via the clock is a challenge: It calls for better instructional strategies, tools, and management. "Time can be considered an absolute factor that affects a given learning experience. The allocation of time is the single most controllable, and therefore, one of the most powerful operational decisions a school can make" (Ryan, 1991). According to Oakes (1985), time emerges as a pivotal element in the effectiveness of an institution.

Research on the Effects of Time

Bloom (1984) wrote that time on task is one of the variables that accounts for learning differences between students, between classes, and even between nations (Figure 7.1).

Although, in a general sense, it is always better to have more allotted time to increase the prospects of engaged time, within the lesson itself timing and pacing of activities are crucial. Student achievement depends in great measure on the efficient use of every moment in the classroom. The secret of effective learning is thus to increase time on task (to keep students engaged in learning activities) in each lesson, reducing nonlearning time to a minimum (Serdyukov and Serdyukova 2006). Therefore, optimal time planning of all lesson activities may contribute to a more efficient use of the limited lesson time frame and produce improved learning outcomes.

The issue of learning time efficiency is certainly not new. There have been studies of time expenditure in school that demonstrated the importance of effective time management for successful learning outcomes. The three trends that seem to follow from these studies are to:

1. Add time to learning
2. Use the same amount of time while continuing to upgrade both instruction and learning outcomes
3. Try to achieve the same or better learning outcomes in less time (Boyes, Reid, et al. 2004; Kitaigorodskaya 1995; Lozanov 1977; Serdyukov 1984).

● **FIGURE 7.1**

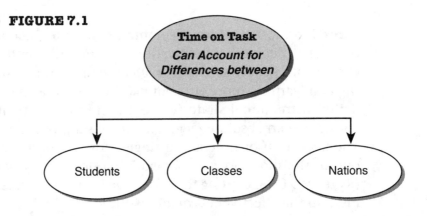

These three trends may look quite contradictory to each other:

1. *More time:* There is an understandable tendency in schools, in view of knowledge growth, diversification, and specialization, to introduce new content areas (courses) or extend the length of existing courses. Is allocating more time to study an answer to improving knowledge management? There is evidence (Scott and Conrad 1992) that increasing learning time does not produce a significant improvement in learning outcomes. Adding time, according to Metzer (2003), does not enhance learning nor does it have a profound effect on the quality of learning outcomes, yet it does raise the cost of study. Increasing time for study will be costly for students, schools, employers, and taxpayers.

2. *Same time:* Making learning more efficient in the same time frame is certainly reasonable; it calls for better instructional strategies, tools, and management.

   > Time is something we cannot control, but you can certainly rationally and effectively organize the use of it. It is the issue of planning and organizing the process. Using the time effectively now provides the opportunity to use the saved time later (Barkley 1999). So, continuously saving time develops a stable habit which eventually may lead to raising productivity of learning. It should be added that efficient use of the learning time together with optimal planning and organizing, requires a more effective instructional methodology and better teacher preparation. (Serdyukov 2005)

3. *Less time:* Contracting or compressing the learning time, though illogical at first look, may be a proactive solution. The goal here is to achieve higher learner productivity and make education more time efficient, hence a great interest for accelerated and other short-term instruction. Various approaches and methodologies for providing education in a shorter time without compromising its academic quality have been described in literature (Bowling, Ries & Ivanitskaya 2002, Boyes, Reid et al. 2004; Scott & Conrad 1992; Serdyukov 1984). The most popular is accelerated learning (AL) that is essentially a compressed, short-term course format. One of the fundamental premises underpinning the potential for acceleration or intensity of learning is that the pacing of educational programs must be responsive to the competencies and knowledge of the individual learner (Robinson & Robinson, 1982). Another premise maintains the idea that people have more intellectual potential for learning than traditional educational

formats can make use of (Lozanov 1977). Building on the principles derived from cognitive psychology, it can be argued that acceleration has the possibility to enhance creativity, outstanding achievement, and higher-order thinking skills (Boyes, Reid et al. 2004). On the other hand, uneconomical ways of managing the learning process and time can reduce actual learning time and interfere with producing the desired learning outcomes (Serdyukov and Serdyukova 2006).

One of the purposes of school is to prepare children for real life. Among other things, school helps develop learning skills together with self-management, which includes time-management skills (Serdyukov & Hill, 2005). Students should know how to become effective independent learners, which implies they need to learn how to organize and manage their time. Learning to use time efficiently during lessons and when doing homework will make students more effective learners, which will serve them well in the real world. One of the teacher's tasks, then, is to identify and evaluate student time-management habits and develop productive ways to increase time efficiency in the learning process.

Timing Lesson Activities

An accurate allocation of time for activities during lesson planning is critical for the lesson plan's successful implementation. You need to calculate how long each activity should take and write the number of minutes for each of the activities. This will allow you to see if you have planned the lesson optimally and can fit everything in. The factors affecting time allocation are as follows:

- Goals and objectives
- The number of activities you need to implement to have students achieve the planned objectives
- The volume of new material
- Class variables (number of students in the class, student preparedness, time of day)
- Your experience

If during the lesson you have a plan with time benchmarks to follow, you will feel more confident in achieving the desired outcomes of the lesson. Certainly, you cannot follow your plan precisely minute to minute because there may be variable circumstances, such as more time spent on student questions during new material presentation or students requiring more time for solving a problem or completing a project. Nevertheless, if you try to remain on schedule, you have the best opportunity to complete the planned activities.

Coming to Terms over Time Management and Lesson Variables

Time, as we have shown, is a crucial factor in education: Any program, course, or lesson is limited in time. Time is a critical teaching constraint, limiting all your intentions and implementations. It is also one of the major factors of success of an organized activity. Remember that, without assigning time values to planned activities and without sticking to them whenever possible, there will be little chance of attaining your goals and reaching the outcomes.

A high school lesson, for example, is usually 50 minutes long. This is why a lesson plan and its components must be assigned weighted time for their implementation, so that the teacher can fulfill the plan and achieve the desired goals and outcomes. In lesson preparation you normally calculate the time you intend to spend on each of the planned activities. You write these time values near every point of the plan so that you can:

- Achieve the objectives set for each of the procedures
- Fulfill the plan on time without compromising the quality of learning
- Feel confident and on task

For instance:

- Presenting the new topic: introduction, reading the text, Q&A, discussion, video demonstration—18 min.
- Student activities: small group work (solving problems)—10 min.
- Student presentations—15 min.
- Assessment—5 min
- Closure—2 min.

● WHAT'S THE PLAN?

When preparing a lesson plan, consider how much time you will allocate to the following procedures. (**Hint:** *Think of the various activities you should select to achieve your planned outcomes.*)

Introduction _____

New material presentation _____

Basic activities _____

Practice _____

Assessment and evaluation _____

Closure _____

> *Optimal time management contributes to the lesson effectiveness.*

Timing, as well as lesson planning and its implementation, may be affected by a few variables that need to be taken into account in the preparation phase:

- *Class size* has an impact on the number of activities to be implemented, the structure of group collaborative activities, time allocation for various activities, amount of information to present, and classroom management.
- Knowledge of student stratification (such as prior knowledge or readiness) is needed for assigning individual tasks and for organizing collaborative work. A helpful solution might be to place students at different developmental levels into heterogeneous small groups. This will ensure better results if peer tutoring and buddy support are used.

- Students' individual characteristics must be considered: Age, culture, language, attention span, learning styles, interests, habits, manners, and personal experiences influence the choice of assignments, tasks and activities, roles to play, and communication modes.
- Availability of instructional tools, including technological ones, and materials is a factor.
- Consider the interval between the previous and the current lesson; in the case of an extended period between the classes, a review of the previously learned material may be necessary.
- Time of day is an issue; people have different perception and attention levels at various times of the day (for instance, the first and the last lessons of the day can be the least productive, while the lessons in the middle of the morning, usually the third and fourth lessons, can be the most productive).

● WHAT'S THE PLAN?

When preparing a lesson plan, consider your class variables. (**Hint:** *Think of how you are going to accommodate the plan according to the following.*)

Class size: _____

Individual characteristics:

_____

_____

Previous lesson on the topic taught . . . days ago, needs review:

_____

_____

Time of day the lesson will be taught:

_____

_____

Time for Self-Directed Learning

Let's turn to the challenge of independent planning, management, and self-control. Independent or self-directed learning can be defined as "a process in which individuals take the initiative, with or without the help of others" (Knowles 1975, p. 11), to diagnose their learning needs, formulate learning goals, identify resources for learning, select and implement learning strategies, and evaluate learning outcomes (Buchler 2003). Self-directed learners are students who take responsibility for their own learning: they take charge and are self-regulated. Students, however, need the teacher to help them realize the importance of effective time management in becoming self-directed learners (Figure 7.2).

Learning time efficiency is a critical factor for learners. The theoretical foundation of effective learning is validated as a result of greater student effort generated in response to improved time expenditures. Such an effort requires effective student time management. Students' self-efficacy is positively related to achievement. It seems clear that a "can-do" attitude on the part of the student is necessary for education to have its most potent effect. Improving learning time efficiency may

● **FIGURE 7.2**

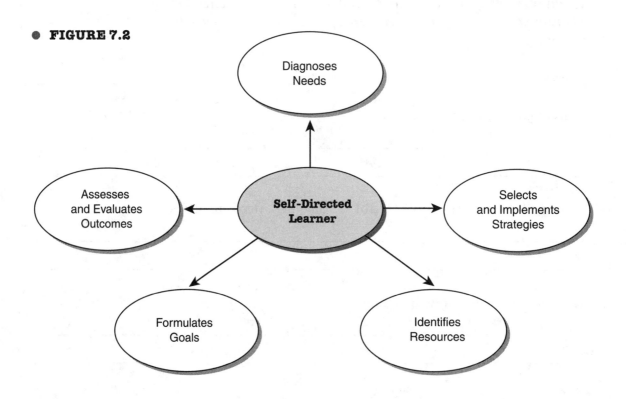

lead to better learning outcomes and a considerable saving of time and energy, thus making education more productive. Students should be made aware of how to time their own learning experiences. Perhaps mentioning your planning strategies as a teacher will set an environment where students can learn to organize their time. In this way, they can set up their own effective study system to be engaged in the learning process and maximize effort over a shorter period of time than is usually required to achieve successful results.

● WHAT'S THE PLAN?

When preparing a lesson plan, consider timing your and student activities:

Presentation of new material: _____ min.

Student basic activities: _____ min.

Student advanced activities: _____ min.

Assessment and evaluation: _____ min.

Introduction and closure: _____ min.

Time Logs

To make your planning more effective and understand how students use their time, ask your students to record how much time they spend on particular activities (Figure 7.3). They can record time by lessons, by days, and by weeks. Then you can combine different student logs and calculate average time spent by activity. After that, you can organize group work in the class, asking students to analyze the data and come up with their evaluation of time usage and ideas for using time more efficiently. This information will also give you the opportunity to rethink your own lesson planning strategies.

● **FIGURE 7.3**

A Log of Student Time

Activities	Time (in Hours)		
	Lesson	Day	Week
1. Preparing for the class (without homework)			
2. Actual time in class			
3. Homework			
4. Out-of-class activities			
5. Reading books			
6. Sports			
7. Playing with children			
8. Communicating with peers outside school			
9. Time spent with parents			
10. Communicating with the teacher			

● **W H A T ' S   T H E   P L A N ?**

When preparing a lesson plan, think how much time your students need to effectively accomplish a given assignment and activity. (*Hint: Think of the time they normally spend on it and try to identify where and how they might save time.*)

_____

_____

_____

Teaching Time

To cope with the challenges of education in the twenty-first century, instructors have to come up with new, effective strategies of facilitating, guiding, and assisting students, while the students have to be taught to develop effective time-management skills. This will help both learners and teachers to successfully cope with the educational tasks and problems within certain time constraints to enhance learning productivity.

As we know, reflection helps teachers understand what they do effectively in the class and where they fail. Reflection includes analysis of your teaching strategies, your teaching style, relationships and communication with students, and, of course, the efficient use of time on various activities.

● WHAT'S THE PLAN?

As you are developing a lesson plan, think how much time you should allocate to each of the planned activities. (**Hint:** *Think of the time you really need to spend.*)

_____

_____

_____

_____

_____

_____

To better understand how efficiently you spend your time, record the time on various activities for a lesson, a day, and a week. Fill in your planned time and then the actual time spent (Figure 7.4).

When you compare your actual time spent versus the planned time, assess the difference. This will tell you about effective ways of managing time.

● **FIGURE 7.4**

A Log of Teacher Time

Activities	Time Expenses (in Hours)		
	Lesson Planned/Actual	Day Planned/Actual	Week Planned/Actual
1. Preparing for teaching			
2. Actual teaching			
3. Field activities			
4. Classroom management			
5. Reading student work			
6. Professional development			
7. Communicating with students outside the classroom			
8. Communicating with parents			
9. Communicating with peers			
10. Communicating with administrators and support			
11. Participating in meetings			

By making the learning process more effective through minimizing waste of the learning time, we may expect more learning to take place in less time, which will result in achieving the planned outcomes with greater efficiency. The formula of effective learning thus is:

The more time sensitive, organized and effective the instructional system, the more opportunities for the student to be engaged in the learning process, the greater the effort and concomitant achievement.

It is worthwhile to make students understand that they are ultimately responsible for their learning. The classroom can provide an instructor-facilitated learning environment, but to sustain success, students must become more and more self-directed learners with each day.

Time in an Asynchronous Environment

When we leave the traditional classroom and consider the late twentieth and early twenty-first century phenomenon of online education, we can see how many of the seemingly immutable facets of time are changed via the concept of **asynchronous design,** where there is no precise timing needed to communicate. Because online education uses computers that access the Internet, communication (e-mail, threaded discussions, formal essays) can be archived. This allows extra time for the learner to learn at his or her own pace—and for you to read, respond, and grade student work without a strict time limit.

In terms of providing time for reflective thought, asynchronous design appears to be inherently superior to the synchronicity of the traditional classroom. Recall the notion that how we learn determines what we learn. The power of the "how" in learning, or what we call the methodology, cannot be underestimated. For example, let's travel back to the 1890s. If you wanted to hear the music of John Philip Sousa and his popular U.S. Marine Band, you had very limited options. Unless you had a treadle-powered graphophone and had access to Edison and/or Columbia cylinders (the CDs of their time), you had to go to wherever Sousa's band was playing. Even then, you could only listen to what Sousa chose to play. Moreover, unless there was an encore, you could only hear a song once in a performance. Compare that to today, where you can download Sousa marches on your computer to your heart's content and listen whenever you want and as many times as you want.

Now consider the difference between the late nineteenth and early twenty-first centuries. It is the difference between synchronous and asynchronous design. In short, listening to a specific artist, being at a specific place, waiting for the specific time for a single performance or having access to not only Sousa but virtually an unlimited number of musical artists and musical performances wherever you want increases your opportunities to enjoy music. Students or teachers can now connect to the Internet, an iPod, or other mobile technology

● **FIGURE 7.5**

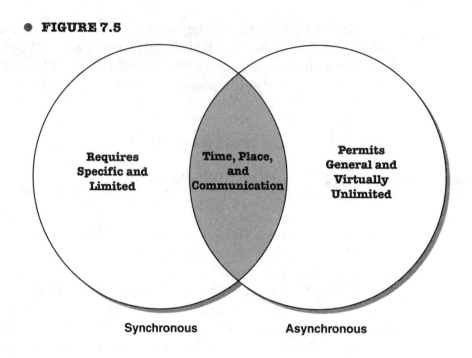

accessing curricular information or communicating whenever they wish, experiencing imagery and sound as many times as they desire. The opportunities for learning at one's own pace are greater today than ever before (Figure 7.5).

Viewed as a learning tool, technology that allows for asynchronous design is pedagogically superior to a "live" synchronous performance—and ultimately presents learners (with a multiplicity of learning styles) more ways to understand. Asynchronicity inherently provides more flexibility and opportunities to learn via various modalities.

Understanding time as an organizing principle in the classroom is a precondition to an in-depth discussion of knowledge construction and skill development. Organizing, structuring, and modeling in the classroom have little value without time. Planning also affects how you teach and how students learn. Consequently, an effective lesson plan sets an environment for interactive learning and an enhanced educational outcome.

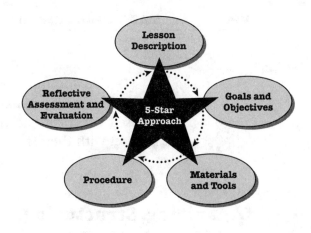

CHAPTER 8

....

Knowledge Construction and Skill Development

A *lesson plan is a product, and planning a lesson is a process. As a product, a lesson plan provides a knowledge base and concomitant skills. As a process, planning a lesson ensures a systematic way to achieve success in the classroom (for example, learning to read and then reading to learn). A reliable lesson plan can make the teaching and learning experience one of active engagement.*

Coming to Terms over Organizing, Structuring, and Modeling in Education

....

You probably realize that education is organized learning. To organize learning requires planning, and the latter is the foundation of education. Creating a lesson plan involves planning for learning experiences. **Lesson planning** helps to structure instruction, learning, classroom practice, and your time. This eventually makes your teaching performance more efficient, less stressful, and, what is crucial, rewarding for you. Most importantly, a well-constructed lesson plan sets a pathway to learning for your students.

Thorough lesson plan development is a precondition for effective teaching. The 5-Star Lesson Plan is designed to make your teaching performance smoother and at the same time less time consuming.

All educational programs are designed according to plans, and these strategies emanate from your curriculum. A successful plan provides for a highly reliable learning process and permits achievement of your goals.

Does planning affect a teacher's professional behavior? It certainly does, as research and experience show: Planning helps teachers remain focused on the topic they are teaching, affecting the way teachers interact with their students and improving learning outcomes.

Organizing, Structuring, and Modeling in Education

Modeling, or simulation, is another side of organization and structuring. When you prepare a lesson, you actually create a lesson prototype, an organizational structure of an instructional process you are going to implement in your class. If you look at the lesson plan you have just developed from this perspective, you will realize that it is actually a model of your future lesson (Serdyukov 2002). It will define not only the what, how, and when of your lesson but also the time allotted to structured classroom activities.

What, then, is a **structured classroom activity?** It is a major element of your plan and a basic unit of organized learning. Of course, an activity within a lesson plan may be also a model of knowledge application in practice. For example, when you teach English Language Learners (ELL) how to communicate in English, you teach them to do it through communicative exercises that imitate real communication. You set realistic communicative tasks and create circumstances that would simulate real-life situations. Then you engage the ELL learner in performing these tasks.

For example, in teaching students to make acquaintances, you first demonstrate how you introduce yourself and then model this activity with one of the more advanced students. Then you give the class the following assignments:

1. Introduce yourself to your neighbor on the left.
2. Introduce yourself to your neighbor on the right.
3. Ask your neighbor on the right to introduce you to your neighbor on the left.
4. Introduce your neighbor on the left to your neighbor on the right.
5. Introduce yourself to the class.
6. Ask your neighbor on the right about your neighbor on the left.

7. Ask your neighbor on the left about other people in the class.

8. You are at a reception. Try to meet as many people as you can. Don't forget to introduce yourself each time you meet other people.

9. Make up a list of all those present in the room.

In this simulated activity, going through several cycles or iterations, students will be trying to achieve their pragmatic communicative goals in actual conversation in the target language. The objectives are not simply to memorize new words and patterns (mere information) but to engage the learners in meaningful person-to-person interactions (procedures leading to skill development). This is how second or foreign language skills should be developed.

When you give your students assignments in the classroom, see that these assignments are related to the students' background and potential application in real life. For instance, if you want your students to talk about food, you can set an atmosphere where students express genuine interest in doing a particular assignment by suggesting they are hungry and you are going to take them to a (virtual) restaurant. Show them a video clip about a restaurant or a couple of slides showing restaurant views; then give them menus from the restaurant and suggest that they order food according to their liking. If you role play, breaking the class into pairs where one student will play the role of a customer and the other will be a waiter, you will generate a fun activity with very effective outcomes.

● WHAT'S THE PLAN?

As you think about lesson plan strategies and activities, what, in your opinion, is the difference between transmitting information and engaging the student in a meaning-centered activity? (**Hint:** *Think of the distinction between mere information and meaning—which do you think better engages the student?*)

_____

_____

_____

_____

_____

Modeling/simulation is a technique we often use in education. For example, when you teach your students to cooperate and collaborate while solving learning tasks, you not only help them construct new knowledge but also model real-life, collaborative, problem-solving situations that they will encounter more than once in their future jobs.

When you present a new topic, material, or problem, you try whenever possible to construct or imitate a practical example. Thus, if you teach math or physics, you demonstrate how problem solving can be applied to real-life tasks through using a model of an actual situation. When you teach English as a second language (ESL) or some foreign language, you help your students to master patterns of the target language use: typical colloquialisms and expressions, standard phrases, and sample dialogues.

● WHAT'S THE PLAN?

As you think about lesson plan strategies and activities, ponder the relationship between the lesson and the student's own prior knowledge. Write down an activity that you believe will "connect" with your students. (**Hint:** *To make your curriculum culturally responsive, you need to model a real-life situation that relates to the background that the students bring to the class.*)

_____

_____

_____

_____

_____

_____

Last but not least, everything you do in class verbally or nonverbally, emotionally or cognitively sets a model. In other words, what and how you behave, communicate, and interact, inherently sets a model that students will, for better or worse, consciously or unconsciously, imitate.

Many of us have fond memories of a favorite teacher. In choosing a teaching career we now realize what a profound impact he or she may have had on our lives. That is the power of modeling. We remember that former teacher not only as a competent instructor but also as a caring human being. Education to a great extent is modeling. Organizing, planning, structuring, and modeling are some of the "secrets" of a quality education.

● WHAT'S THE PLAN?

According to research, 80 percent of teaching is modeling. What are the traits you wish to model in class?

_____

_____

_____

_____

_____

_____

Other Approaches to Lesson Planning

There have been quite a few attempts to design an effective lesson plan structure. One of the best known is Madeline Hunter's seven-step lesson plan (Hunter 1995), which in some aspects is different from our 5-Star Lesson Plan. Hunter's steps are as follows:

1. Objectives
2. Standards
3. Anticipatory set
4. Presentation
5. Guided practice
6. Independent practice
7. Closure

This seven-step lesson plan does not specifically mention an important component of a lesson—the reflective assessment and evaluation of students' performance and outcomes. Homework assignments and homework checkup missing here are two other important phases of the lesson that should also be included in an effective plan. Finally, an introduction is needed in the beginning of the lesson to initiate the lesson for students and prepare them for learning.

The lesson plan, while the main focus of this workbook, does not function in isolation. Instead it is a vital part of the learning process that emanates from prior lesson plans or prior student knowledge and leads to yet another lesson. The lesson plan is a link in a chain of learning that connects one idea to another. Now let's consider how we are going to achieve intended learning outcomes via strategic and tactical planning.

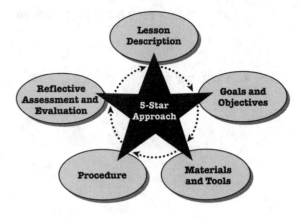

CHAPTER 9

Course and Lesson: Strategic and Tactical Planning

Understanding short- and long-range planning and how your lesson plan fits into a sequence of lessons to present new knowledge and skills while reinforcing previous learning is part of a well-planned learning process that can become your modus operandi for delivering the most enriched curricula to all students while using the widest variety of methodological approaches.

Coming to Terms over a Lesson in the Course

Besides discussing a lesson plan, let us take a look at the position a lesson occupies in a course. A **course** delivering a certain subject matter or specific content represents a particular area that can be considered as a whole. The **lessons in a course** are its constituent parts, each of them being derived from another and dependent on the others. In the instructional process they extend sequentially through a certain period of time (a year, a semester, a quarter, a month, a week, or a day) and together form a complete single whole, both as a system and as a continuum.

A course can be broken into course structure blocks commonly united by a topic. These blocks are called units. A unit consists of several lessons. So, a course as a system has a hierarchical structure (see Figure 9.1).

● FIGURE 9.1

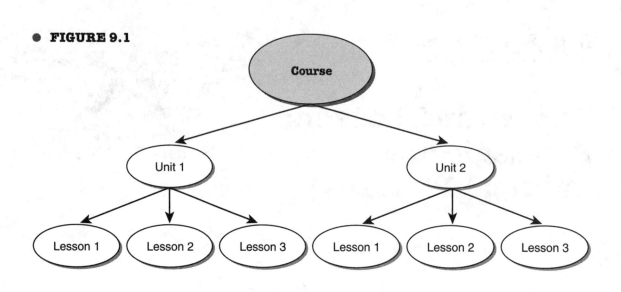

As a process, a course is a sequence of lessons that unwrap one by one along a time line. This is a continuous process that begins when the course goals and objectives are stated and ends when the learners' outcomes are assessed and evaluated. Thus, each course can also be described as a linear sequence of lessons (see Figure 9.2).

A single lesson consequently can be presented as a sequence of various activities, both teacher's and students', organized around the lesson goal and objectives by a plan.

While working on a lesson plan, it is important to remember that a lesson is not a stand-alone piece in the course: It is just one section of the process, and it is usually devoted to a particular topic; it naturally stems from the previous lesson and, at the same time, lays down the foundation for the subsequent lesson.

● FIGURE 9.2

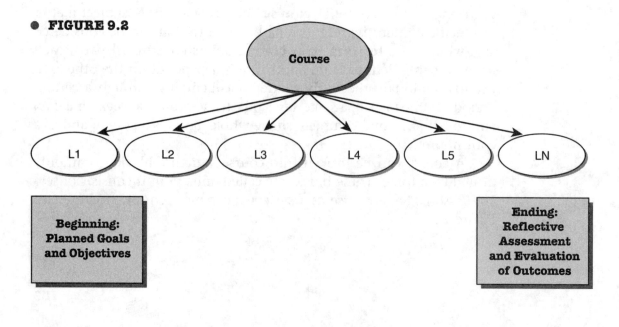

● WHAT'S THE PLAN?

Give an example of a lesson plan that links to the previous lesson and creates a bridge to a future lesson.

_____

_____

_____

_____

That is why, when developing a lesson plan, we have to take into account the lesson's position in the course system. As a part of a sequence, it provides connections to both the previous and subsequent lesson in the course.

Therefore, we can talk of two kinds of planning: **strategic planning** is a long-range design of a particular course (for example, math may be taught differently than is English literature). On the other hand, **tactical planning** is a short-range design focusing on the different aspects planning a lesson (for example, the 5-Star Lesson Plan).

These two kinds of planning have different rules. Here we focus on tactical planning. However, it will be beneficial for you to keep in mind the strategic aspects of planning. So, try to maintain links to the previous lesson, when you start a new one, by reviewing it or referring to its main points. In addition, try also to make projections for the next lesson when concluding the present lesson.

An Algorithm of a Lesson Plan

A lesson plan can be presented in the form of an algorithm (linear, branching, or iterative) using the "If . . . then . . ." logical formula. An **algorithm** is a predetermined set of operations leading to an intended outcome. A medical prescription or a cooking recipe is in essence an algorithm. An example of the iterative algorithm for a homework checkup activity is presented in Figure 9.3.

The algorithmic procedure is implemented as follows: A homework checkup is an operation in which a teacher checks a student's preparedness for the lesson using various instructional tools such as questions, tests, quizzes, oral reports, and written papers. If the student's homework is found good (yes), the teacher can move on to new material presentation. If the work does not meet preset criteria (no), then

● **FIGURE 9.3**

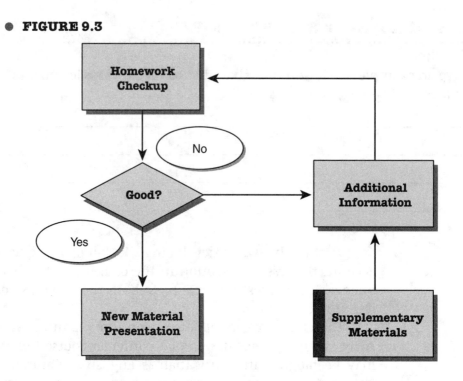

additional instruction is provided that can be supported by supplementary materials and other activities. Thus, the cycle continues until the student passes the checkup satisfactorily.

Actually, this loop represents a classic learning cycle. The procedure is a standard pattern of an instructional process that reflects typical classroom practices.

● WHAT'S THE PLAN?

Considering the algorithmic procedure, how can a you set a successful learning environment? (**Hint:** *Consider reteaching. Recall that your job is to help raise students to meet standards.*)

_____

_____

_____

Learning cycles form an inherent pattern. Patterns are a major element in lesson plan implementation. Any pattern in your lesson plan will not suffice; the step-by-step design of the lesson plan and, as will we see, its implementation must be well-coordinated and congruent.

CHAPTER 10

....

Implementing
the Plan

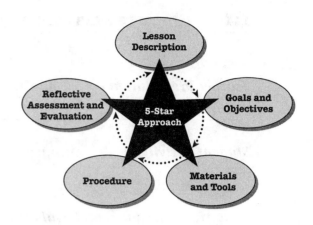

*D*esigning a lesson plan and implementing that plan are tasks that are related yet quite different. Preparing the plan is akin to drawing your own road map to a certain desired destination. Putting that plan into action is like driving the car to your predetermined spot. There are many factors that go into implementing a successful lesson plan: the students who attend your class, the configuration of your classroom, the access you have to teaching and learning materials, and your skilled implementation of instructional approaches. All these figure into your curricular journey to get you where you want to go.

IMPLEMENTATION

Subject: _____

Topic: _____

Grade: _____

Standards: _____

_____

Goal: _____

_____

Objectives: _____

_____

Teacher Presentation (_____ min.): _____

_____

Student Activities (_____ min.): _____

_____

Reflective Assessment and Evaluation (_____ min.): _____

_____

Other Activities (_____ min.): _____

_____

Appreciating Students' Diversity

One of the most important factors to be taken into account in lesson preparation is individual students' characteristics: their diversity—cultural, ethnic, and racial; their special needs; and their psychological individuality—attention, retention, learning style, and behavior. Instructional models appropriate for a culturally, linguistically, and academically diverse student populations should be incorporated into your lesson plans.

The first precondition to democratic education is equal access. This can be achieved through appropriate planning and by using strategies and activities that meet the demands of special needs and second language or English language learners (ELL). The lessons that serve these learners have five major aims:

- Assist students in their needs
- Help ELL students become proficient in English
- Allow them to participate efficiently in the core curriculum
- Support students' positive self-image
- Promote cross-cultural understanding

Such an approach requires effective English language development that aims at achieving CALP (cognitive academic language proficiency—J. Cummins 1979), use of students' primary language and cultural background, sheltered academic instruction, scaffolding, and students' inclusion in the mainstream academic process.

Research indicates that the academic language used in content areas may act as a barrier to the success in school for many ELL students. A critical element in second language development is access to comprehensible input in English.

To make content accessible to ELLs, your goal has to be facilitating the gaining of English proficiency while developing in academic areas. The following strategies can be recommended:

- Slow but natural speech
- Clear enunciation
- Short simple sentences
- Controlled vocabulary
- Visual reinforcement
- Frequent comprehension checks

Some additional planning procedures can be recommended for the lesson intended for ELLs:

- Teaching previously selected vocabulary before presenting new material (presenting new words and illustrating their use in context)
- Preceding written activities by oral activities, such as questions and answers and discussion
- Designing collaborative communicative activities by assigning teams, appropriate roles, and materials
- Using real-life materials and noneducational literature relevant to the topic

An effective contemporary approach to teaching ELLs is SDAIE (Specially Designed Academic Instruction in English), also called sheltered instruction. SDAIE is a synthesis of advanced methodological approaches that have a common purpose of allowing English learners to succeed. Subject matter is delivered in English, whatever the grade level. SDAIE uses language-sensitive strategies, and contextual support and focuses on making instruction in English more comprehensible. Major components of SDAIE are:

- Academically demanding content; authentic, relevant, interesting, and coherent materials and tasks
- Theme-based and student-centered learning; prior knowledge; contextualized instruction; cooperative learning
- Positive affective domain
- Performance-based and authentic assessment

An integrated language teaching approach provides the necessary foundation for successful ELL learning. This approach focuses on using the target language in context rather than just learning the language. Language is presented and developed in compact and meaningful chunks instead of small unrelated elements. Language experience, both oral and written, should be interwoven with the learning in all curricular areas and in all lessons.

● WHAT'S THE PLAN?

When preparing a lesson plan, consider ELL students' English proficiency. (***Hint:*** *Think of how you are going to accommodate the plan according to their level to help them successfully learn the new material.*)

Vocabulary: _____

Your speech: _____

Visuals: _____

Comprehension checks: _____

Activities: _____

Other: _____

Lesson plans that incorporate holistic learning, the combination of the social, emotional, and intellectual aspects of student development, clearly present a transformational model. Holistic learning can be approached through an appreciation of the theory of Multiple Intelligences (MI). Howard Gardner (1993) posits that students possess a number of different intelligences that can be observed as students solve problems. Intelligence, therefore, is the ability to apply one or more intelligences in ways that a certain community or culture finds valuable. MI theory presents a path to comprehend intelligence. Lesson plans that incorporate multiple ways of learning and knowing present activities that reach more students. When students are given choices about how to demonstrate their learning, teachers are transferring some control to students, thus making the process learner centered. The results of that transfer encourage students to build on existing strengths to best comprehend new content and skills.

MI theory works well as a guide to develop lesson plans that meet the needs of a diverse group of learners. The objective is not to teach to a specific intelligence (that is, linguistic, logical/mathematical, visual/spatial, bodily/kinesthetic, musical, naturalistic, interpersonal, intrapersonal), or even to match intelligences with specific activities, but instead to permit learners to use their preferred ways of processing (such as metacognition) and then communicating new learning.

● WHAT'S THE PLAN?

When preparing a lesson plan, consider your students' multiple intelligences. (**Hint:** *Think of how you are going use students' strengths to accommodate the plan.*)

Linguistic: _____

Logical-mathematical: _____

Musical: _____

Bodily-kinesthetic: _____

Interpersonal: _____

Intrapersonal: _____

Spatial: _____

Naturalistic (environmental): _____

State Standards and District Benchmarks

Every state has its own K–12 academic standards and every district its benchmarks. In California, for instance, these standards include curriculum framework, content standards in the subject area, English language development standards, and teacher professional expectations (http://www.ca.gov/cfir/). When planning a lesson, you should address these standards.

● WHAT'S THE PLAN?

When preparing a lesson plan, consider state standards and district benchmarks. (**Hint:** *Go online and select those state standards and district benchmarks that apply to your current lesson.*)

Subject: _____

Topic: _____

Goal: _____

Objectives: _____

_____

Standards: _____

_____

Benchmarks: _____

The Principle of Balance in a Lesson Plan

> *The end should match the beginning.* (Russian Proverb)

An effective lesson plan is a specific systematic educational design aimed at achieving a desired outcome. Like any practical system, to function properly it should be balanced. The balance should be among:

- Structure and function
- Structure and content
- Outcomes and objectives
- Your teaching and student learning
- Group and individual work
- Activities and objectives
- The amount of information to be presented and lesson time constraints

- The amount of information to be presented and the amount of information that can possibly be consumed
- Students' level of preparation and content complexity
- Students' individual idiosyncratic characteristics and developmental tasks
- ESL student proficiency and lesson content
- Special education students' proficiency and lesson content
- Learning performance and assessment
- Outcomes and evaluation

The principle of balance (Serdyukov 2002) stipulates that all components of the lesson plan must be well coordinated and congruent. When there is an imbalance in a lesson plan or its implementation, the lesson goals and objectives can hardly be achieved (for example, when the objectives are not supported by adequate activities or when students' outcomes are not matched by valid evaluation).

● WHAT'S THE PLAN?

When preparing a lesson plan, consider all plan elements and assess them in the context of your whole plan. (***Hint:*** *Try to weigh the elements against the suggested approach and see if your plan is balanced.*)

Outcomes and evaluation _____

Structure and content _____

Your teaching and student learning _____

Activities and objectives _____

Group and individual work _____

The amount of information to be presented and lesson time constraints

_____

The amount of information to be presented and the amount of information that can possibly be consumed

_____

(continued)

Students' level of preparation and content complexity

_____

Students' individual psychological characteristics, assignments, and activities

_____

ELL student proficiency and lesson content   _____

Learning performance and assessment   _____

Lesson Execution

A good lesson plan, however, is not a guarantee of a successful lesson: sound methodological strategies and techniques and a competent and caring teacher are other essential aspects of the lesson implementation.

A lesson is a complex process that has two intermingled sides, preparation/planning and implementation. A lesson plan, thus, is one side of the lesson. The second side is classroom implementation that affects content presentation, students' activities, use of teaching and learning materials, visuals and technology, and application of instructional strategies, methods, and techniques.

It is optimal to prepare students for the next day's lesson by describing the lesson's general outline at the conclusion of the day's lesson, thus setting the anchors, key ideas, or anticipatory points for the future class. Likewise, it is beneficial to return to the previous lesson material in an overview or recapitulation of the major points or issues learned in the preceding lesson in the introductory stage. In this way, the teacher builds a continuity of learning, an interrelated sequence of instructional events, a meaningful logical composition of the content pieces in the students' minds, which ensures better understanding and retention.

The structure of the lesson may vary according to its goals and objectives. There may be variations in the sequence of the stages (for example, activities based on the previously learned material can precede presentation of the new material). Some modules and elements may repeat (for example, presentation or cyclic activities can be reiterated several times during one lesson).

Because students certainly have various learning styles, it is important to have several options for the next day's lesson implementation. An experienced teacher always has a backup set of activities, assignments, and materials for each lesson to prepare for eventualities. There can be additional stages a teacher can introduce in a lesson: a relaxation pause, a physical exercise, a stretching break, a repetition session, a game, or a quiz. Any and all can be included in the lesson process if and when the teacher finds it necessary.

● WHAT'S THE PLAN?

Having taught a lesson, review the plan and see what worked and what did not work. Reflect and analyze lesson effective features and flaws.

_____

_____

_____

_____

_____

_____

_____

_____

_____

_____

_____

_____

_____

_____

_____

_____

Affective Component

We are very well aware of the fact that we learn (as well as do anything else) better when we are interested—in short, when positive emotions are involved. Of all of the factors that go into a quality education, the personal and scholastic rapport involving teachers and their students may be the most significant. The core relationship must be built on trust and a mutual desire for students to reach the twin goals of academic growth and social development.

The **affective domain** involves our emotions and values. Inspiration, motivation, and empowerment, all affective in nature, express our deepest feelings of self-worth and commitment. One's affective disposition is interwoven into one's cognitive ability.

The teacher's emotional behavior, affective conduct, keen interest and involvement with the students, continuous interaction, and communication are crucial for the students' success. The use of humor (your best friend) and the absence of sarcasm or temper (your worst enemy) cannot be underrated. In addition, paralinguistic means of communication—music, visuals, multimedia, play, and collaborative activities—are the warp and woof of a fabric of diverse teaching methods to meet the needs of many distinct learning styles. However, when it comes to affective domain, a teacher's enthusiasm for what is to be taught in the lesson is imperative.

Motivation is a driving force in student learning and is closely connected to the affective domain. Two types of motivation are known, extrinsic and intrinsic, the latter being the more efficient and the more powerful of the two. Let us consider intrinsic motivation as genuine motivation because it resides in the learner. To have a student increase his or her motivation for learning and resulting enhanced achievement, it is vital for the teacher to set an environment where the learner elects to become engaged in goals and objectives. For example, instead of stating the objective as "Students will be able to . . . ," one might say, to personalize the lesson "You will be able to . . ."

Instead of "It is interesting to know," one might posit using analogies to the learner's prior knowledge: "You will be amazed to know that it will help you each day when you . . ." Besides the personalized goals, role playing is extremely useful in developing an individual student's involvement in collaboration and in learning. Other factors that are beneficial for setting an environment where the students choose to become engaged through the whole lesson are:

- Interesting and relevant content
- Engaging activities
- Enlightened class management
- Use of visuals
- Video materials
- Music
- Appreciation embedded in the curriculum of students ever more culturally and linguistically diverse

● WHAT'S THE PLAN?

When preparing a lesson plan, think of the ways to make your lesson stimulating, setting an environment for students to choose to be motivated while having fun. (**Hint:** *Include humorous stories, visuals, video clips, multimedia presentations, music, songs.*)

_____

_____

_____

Lesson Assessment and Revision

The plan of the lesson is prepared. What next? Should you start teaching? Before you implement the plan, take some time to review and assess it. The actual assessment will certainly be done by the students who can be the most rigorous critics. You will know of it by observing their work in the classroom, by asking questions and assessing their performance. Still, it is worthwhile to give a preliminary educated guess of the lesson and its parts while it is on paper. How? First, the principle of balance can be applied to see if the projected outcomes will meet the objectives. Then criteria for the preassessment might be applied. They include the following points:

1. *Logical structure of the plan:* Each subsequent module and activity must stem from the previous one, while keeping in mind the overall plan of the course, and be linked to the subsequent module and activity.

2. *Activities:* Is there a sufficient number of activities to provide for reaching the objectives? Are they well organized into a consistent system of learning?

3. *Time evaluation for each activity during the lesson:* Do I have sufficient time to implement all items of my plan? Do I use the time efficiently?.

4. *Accessibility of teaching and learning materials.*

5. *Availability of a contingency plan:* In case you run out of time, you have some time left, or you have fewer students than you planned for—what would you do?

6. *Classroom preparedness.*

7. *Classroom management techniques*

You can also use the following checklist to preassess your lesson:

- Did I include academic content standards? Are they appropriate for this lesson and for my students?
- Did I clearly state the goal and objectives?
- Do the subject matter, language material, cognitive demands, and activities fit into previous knowledge and experiences as well as students' abilities?
- Will I be able to make the input and learning materials comprehensible?
- How will I take into account students' first languages and cultures?
- Did I integrate all the four language skills into the lesson activities?
- Did I take into account students' multiple intelligences and learning styles?
- Will there be sufficient time for students' individual and collaborative activities, communication, questions, and interaction with the materials?
- Do I have sufficient visuals, realia, and manipulatives?
- Will I make a good use of available technologies?
- Did I include formal and informal assessment and evaluation procedures?
- Will I be able to implement everything I planned in the allocated time frame?

When the lesson has been taught, take time to revise its implementation, reflect, and find out where you faltered or where the plan had been impractical. Make a list of both positive and negative notes and try to introduce the necessary corrections to the previous version of your plan for future applications. Use time logs (see Chapter 7) and analyze your use of time in the lesson. Next time, when you teach the same lesson, you will be fully prepared. Remember: Reflection is one of the major instruments of a teacher's professional growth.

● WHAT'S THE PLAN?

When preparing a lesson plan, consider your own criteria for preassessment. (***Hint:*** *Select the most critical factors.*)

_____

_____

_____

_____

Teacher's Lesson Collection

In the course of planning and teaching, every teacher collects a great number of plans and various teaching materials for his or her course. It is very convenient to save and maintain the collection of lesson plans and various materials for your subject area or a particular course. A teacher's lesson collection (TELECOL) is a complete set of plans developed for each lesson, together with teaching materials such as texts, visuals, handouts that can be copied as needed, videoclips, computer-based materials, Web links to parts of the lesson, and so on, that the teacher uses in the classroom. This collection is always ready for you to access.

TELECOL may be invaluable when you need a substitute teacher for your class. You can give a complete package for a lesson to your substitute, who will then teach along your guidelines using your model and the materials that will guarantee maintenance of your teaching model and quality of work. This collection, certainly, needs to be reviewed, updated, and replenished continuously.

A teacher's lesson collection provides the educator with a complete and reliable bank of teaching materials that make teaching easily replicable and, as such, more technological and efficient.

A Checklist for Your Lesson Collection
- Lesson plans
- Content (textbook)
- Additional materials for the content delivery:
  Books, texts, printouts

  > Visuals (pictures, albums, wall posters, maps, slides, transparencies)

  > Video (tapes, courses, clips, CDs, DVDs)

  > Realia and manipulatives (objects, models, toys)

  > Games (jigsaw puzzles, dominoes, playing cards)

  > Multimedia (computer courseware)

  > Web links to relevant sites
- Technology (computer, DVD and CD players, Internet hookup, slide projector, overhead projector, TV, tape recorder, video camera)
- Handouts (texts, charts, tables)

- Activities bank
    - Activities and their descriptions
    - Games
    - Other materials for activities
- Assessment bank (questionnaires, rubrics)
- Evaluation bank (quizzes and tests, including computerized ones)
- Samples of students' work

● WHAT'S THE PLAN?

Make up a list of your teaching collection.

_____

_____

_____

_____

_____

_____

_____

_____

_____

_____

_____

_____

_____

_____

Your Turn: Practice Sheets

I. IMPLEMENTATION

Subject: _____

Topic: _____

Grade: _____

Standards: _____

_____

Goals: _____

_____

Objectives: _____

_____

Teacher Presentation (_____ min.): _____

_____

Student Activities (_____ min.): _____

_____

Reflective Assessment and Evaluation (_____ min.): _____

_____

Other Activities (_____ min.): _____

_____

II. IMPLEMENTATION

Subject: _____

Topic: _____

Grade: _____

Standards: _____

_____

Goals: _____

_____

Objectives: _____

_____

Teacher Presentation (_____ min.): _____
_____

Student Activities (_____ min.): _____
_____

Reflective Assessment and Evaluation (_____ min.): _____
_____

Other Activities (_____ min.): _____
_____

III. IMPLEMENTATION

Subject: _____

Topic: _____

Grade: _____

Standards: _____
_____

Goals: _____
_____

Objectives: _____
_____

Teacher Presentation (_____ min.): _____
_____

Student Activities (_____ min.): _____
_____

Reflective Assessment and Evaluation (_____ min.): _____
_____

Other Activities (_____ min.): _____
_____

IV. IMPLEMENTATION

Subject: _____

Topic: _____

Grade: _____

Standards: _____

_____

Goals: _____

_____

Objectives: _____

_____

Teacher Presentation (_____ min.): _____

_____

Student Activities (_____ min.): _____

_____

Reflective Assessment and Evaluation (_____ min.): _____

_____

Other Activities (_____ min.): _____

_____

V. IMPLEMENTATION

Subject: _____

Topic: _____

Grade: _____

Standards: _____

_____

Goals: _____

_____

Objectives: _____

_____

Teacher Presentation (_____ *min.):* _____

_____

Student Activities (_____ *min.):* _____

_____

Reflective Assessment and Evaluation (_____ *min.):* _____

_____

Other Activities (_____ *min.):* _____

_____

Now that we have discussed implementing the lesson plan, let's think about the application of your plan not only in the classroom but in the real world, where students spend most of their time. One powerful way to best apply your plan is to access your students' families as the human resources you need to extend the school day. Another critical element in your plan is blending standards-based curricula via the social aspects of community life with approaches like service learning. By putting academics in action, young citizens not only know their rights but act on their duty to the community.

Extending the Lesson Plan to Home

ducation is a family as well as a societal affair. To best educate a child, every resource a teacher can access proves useful in reinforcing that youngster's educational experience. Because of the limited time that students actually spend in school, your lesson plans need to involve your pupils' families. This chapter will explain the imperative aspect of a learning triangle made up of the student, the parent/family, and you, the teacher. One of the best ways to extend the learning process of your lesson is to engage students in serving their community.

The First and Most Important Teachers

In the preceding chapters we have outlined the why, what, and how of effective lesson plans. We have seen how lesson plans lay out a blueprint for successful teaching and learning. Having said that, you can have a well-prepared teacher, a well-thought-out lesson plan, and a sincere student who genuinely tries to achieve—and still get failure from that equation.

Why does American education fail so often? Why is it that only 70 percent of ninth graders graduate with their class? Why is that about half of all African American and Latino students do not graduate from high school?

To begin to answer this question, we must look to the first and most important teachers in the life of a child—the parents. Did you know that a typical student spends only 9 percent of his or her time in school from kindergarten through twelfth grade? In other words, it is a fact that a child from 5 years of age to young adulthood at 18 years of age spends 91 percent of his or her time outside the classroom (Figure 11.1).

● **FIGURE 11.1**

Time Spent in School K–12

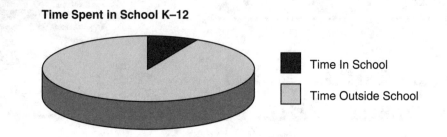

■ Time In School

□ Time Outside School

We are sure asking a lot from that 9 percent of the time in the classroom! There is an African saying that it takes a community to educate a child. Resources outside the school can make a difference inside the school. There can be no doubt that, in the exchange of communication between the teacher and the parents as to what is being taught and how, parents can play a part in reflective assessment that is of critical importance. The traditional one-on-one duo of teacher and student has not proven successful in too many cases. What is called for is a triangular configuration of parent, student, and teacher (Figure 11.2).

To make best use of this limited time frame in school, your lesson plans must involve the parents and/or family (including guardians, grandmothers and grandfathers, brothers and sisters) in the day-to-day learning process. In today's real world of single- or even absent-parent families and latchkey children, a teacher must find that third party in our triangle. Many times it will be a grandmother or other adult relative, sometimes it will be an older brother or sister. Older brothers or sisters many times will not only take on the responsibility of looking after their younger sibling but see right through a younger child's excuses because they do not have to battle through the generation gap!

● **FIGURE 11.2**

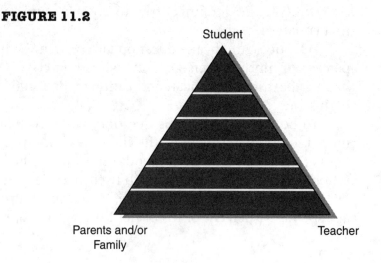

Student

Parents and/or
Family

Teacher

● **FIGURE 11.3**

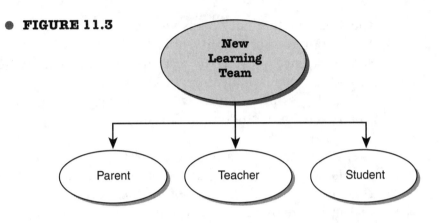

What is important is to find that other person who truly cares about the student (Figure 11.3).

Involving the parents and/or family in the learning process is the kind of engagement that opens parents' access to monitoring the academic development and social growth of their sons and daughters. It also provides the teacher with important feedback about the child because parents have unique information about the child that the teacher may never know without the parent's assistance. It also gives the opportunity for the teacher and parents to assure a coordinated and straightforward message to the child about the importance and value of education.

Academics in Action

Community involvement in the educational process is also critical. Teachers who are able to rally a community to honor education make a real difference in the quality of life, as together with the community they weave an economic and social fabric of hope and inclusion. Economically, students secure better jobs via a good education. Socially, the very essence of American society, a participatory democracy via an educated citizenry, depends on and encourages a more responsive government. Community involvement can amplify and bring credibility to a teacher's lesson so, in the end, young people get a valuable message that can last for a lifetime.

Service learning is both a philosophy and methodological concept that constructs bridges from your lesson plan to the community. This occurs by integrating into your curriculum activities that are mutually rewarding to your students as well as to the community at large. For example, a school poetry festival, where the community is invited to hear the students' original poems written in their English classes, benefits the school, the community, and the young people involved. Likewise, school science projects to test the pollutants in the air and water provide a valuable educational tool to everyone in the community. Significantly, research indicates that service learning curricula have led to an increase in student achievement and a decrease in truancy and vandalism.

When teachers are in the forefront of organizing educational events, such as inviting scholars and outstanding figures from the community to the school room, education becomes inherently more real and more pertinent. Involving students in service learning—where the school's regular curriculum is blended with a service to the community (a poetry festival for an English class activity, or a food drive to use math skills)—students realize that they not only have personal freedom but a public duty to help their communities. Combining academic development with social growth via community involvement begins with a lesson plan that affects students inside the classroom because it is relevant outside the classroom.

An Approach to Homework

We know that successful completion of homework is a major element in improving academic achievement while building stronger family ties. What is called for is not the old hit-or-miss duo of teacher and student, but a new game plan for a team of three made up of the parent(s), teacher, and student.

Let's see how we can recruit and enlist this winning team for every student in your class to keep everyone informed and participating in the educational process.

The Teacher's Checklist for Parent/Family Involvement:

1. Send a list of a month (or longer) of nightly assignments home, to be placed in an easily accessible place for all to see (for example on the refrigerator).

2. Have some assignments involve parents (such as their cultural and linguistic backgrounds or professional knowledge and experiences).

3. Make follow-up phone calls or e-mails to answer parent's questions.

4. Invite parents on a regular basis to see their child work in class.

5. Ask parents to reward effort (as simple and inexpensive as verbal praise) for effort rather than outcome.

6. Send home a portfolio of the student's work on a regular basis so the learner can explain what he or she is doing.

7. Request that parents write (in the language of their choice) or express to you in a way convenient to them their assessment of their child's effort.

8. Visit with parents on a regular basis, either at school or in their home.

9. Organize parents' meetings, like a parents' club, once a month in school.

● WHAT'S THE PLAN?

Planning your lessons in advance, make a list of ten homework assignments you can present to your students who in turn will give a copy to their parents. (**Suggestion:** *Let's demystify homework and instead of making it busy work or drudgery think of creative and fun assignments*).

_____

_____

_____

_____

_____

Let's focus on checklist items 6 and 7. Sending home a portfolio of the student's typical work (including essays, math problems, science papers, history tests) is powerful because it (Figure 11.4):

1. Encourages the student to take responsibility for his or her performance

2. Teaches the value of self-assessment as students reason through their mistakes and problem solve

3. Improves student's communication skills when he or she explains the what, how, and why of his or her work to parents

4. Opens a dialogue between student and parents on the child's number one vocation in life—that of a student

5. Makes some use of that 91 percent of the time outside the classroom to extend the learning day

● **FIGURE 11.4**

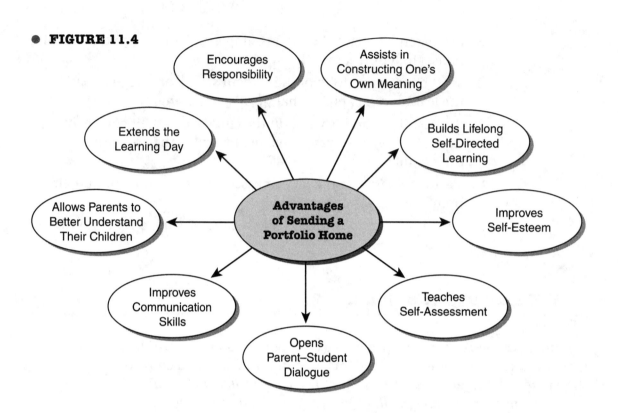

6. Assists students learn to construct their own meanings as they engage with their parents

7. Improves student self-esteem as success builds on success

8. Builds on the ultimate goal of having the student become a lifelong self-directed learner

9. Allows parents to better understand their children by taking their interests to heart

● WHAT'S THE PLAN?

Make a list of the kind of typical graded assignments (remember that those assignments where students do not meet standards should be in the revision process) that you would put in a student's portfolio. (***Hint:*** *Essays and written answers to problems are very valuable in that they demonstrate developing higher order critical thinking skills.*)

_____

_____

_____

_____

_____

It is important to note that the parent does not take the place of the classroom teacher. The parent is there to monitor the work, to be sure it is done, to listen to his or her child's explanation of what is being accomplished, to praise the child's effort, and to communicate back to the teacher his or her opinion of the child's progress via letter, e-mail, phone, or personal visit.

Piaget reasoned that children learn best when given the chance to interact with their environments. It then follows that the greater the interaction between children and their parents (by using a portfolio of accomplishments and homework assignments), the greater the likelihood of student success.

Access to parent/family involvement is also crucial. Today, 45 percent of all U.S. children under 5 years of age come from ethnic minorities. Communication in a culturally pluralistic society made up of many language groups is a daily challenge for many teachers that must be met creatively with resources within the school and the community at large. Finding teacher aides and translators in the neighborhood; at local churches, temples, synagogues, and mosques; and from service organizations in the community is a creative way to bring people together so that parents and teachers as well as parents and their offspring can have an ongoing conversation about the student's academic development and social growth.

● WHAT'S THE PLAN?

What are some of the ways you can reach out to your students of different cultural and linguistic backgrounds? (***Hint:*** *Culturally responsive curricula, in-school bilingual opportunities for every student, and community-based organizations all present wonderful possibilities.*)

_____

_____

_____

_____

_____

_____

_____

Community involvement can take several directions. One of them can take the form of collecting essential information about community life: how the community is structured, what are community centers (services, churches, clubs) and their functions, what are the forms of community activities, how people are organized and participate in the community life. Another direction should be student active engagement in community events: participation in the activities, preparation of public events, helping the sick and poor, cleaning and improving public places.

● **WHAT'S THE PLAN?**

Think of the ways your students can get involved in community life. (**Hint:** *Have students identify various activities and integrate their preparation and/or reporting about them into your lesson plans.*)

_____

_____

_____

_____

Now that the family and the community have been incorporated into your lesson plan to best serve the needs of each and every student you teach, it is time to think about you! Chapter 12 will explore how you can improve as a professional educator and how that can be reflected in your lesson plans.

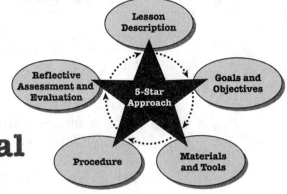

CHAPTER 12

Teacher Professional Competence

A teacher who is competent in the subject matter will still be lacking as a professional educator if he or she does not follow research-based pedagogical principles and does not possess methodological and social skills necessary to work with the learner in a person-to-person learning environment and help that learner through various social, educational, personal, and emotional challenges. Teaching human beings is a multifaceted enterprise.

> *I hear, and I forget. I see, and I remember.*
> *I do, and I understand.* (Confucius)

Coming to Terms over Professional Competence

It goes without saying that quality teaching greatly depends on a teacher's professional competence. Successful lesson plan development is, undeniably, an important part of a teacher's professional capability. What, then, is **professional competence**? It is the ability to perform skillfully on the job.

The teacher's work centers around two major areas:

- Subject matter (for example, mathematics, physics, language, literature)
- Pedagogy (that is, the art and science, or perhaps the craft, of education)

Having noted these two areas it is important to underline that though you may refer to yourself as an "English teacher" or a "second-grade teacher," what you really are is a teacher of human beings. In other words, while you must possess a discerning mind in terms of what you teach and how you teach it, you must also demonstrate a compassionate heart based on your passion to serve every child. This is why the concept of student-centered learning is axiomatic in contempory pedagogy.

To review, the teacher's competence is primarily in two areas, subject matter and pedagogy. These two competences embrace not only sound knowledge in these fields but also a capacity to help students acquire certain information. In addition, students should be able to apply this information in real-life situations. To do this, a teacher has to develop various teaching skills and techniques.

● WHAT'S THE PLAN?

What skills and techniques do you bring to teaching? (**Hint:** *Think of your field of expertise and the "people skills" you have developed*).

_____

_____

_____

_____

_____

_____

_____

However, we know all too well that the teacher's work is very complex and multifaceted. So, besides teaching in his or her subject area, a teacher has to be prepared to deal with various social, cultural, and personal problems both in and outside class and be able to effectively communicate with students and their parents.

One of the greatest disappointments in the life of a student must be when a teacher cannot answer the student's questions about the things that excite that pupil. Last but not least: the teacher's oral and written expression should model a highly literate person—a person who cares about not only *what* he or she says but *how* he or she says it.

It is also critical for a teacher to be a well-rounded person, knowing history, geography, literature; understanding music and art—in short, an interesting human being capable of engaging students.

Five Fundamental Competences

Therefore, we can describe teacher professional competence as a system consisting of five fundamental competences (Serdyukov 2002):

- Expertise in the subject area
- Pedagogical competence
- Sociocultural competence
- Communicative competence
- General erudition

Let us discuss these competences, illustrated in Figure 12.1:

1. Expertise in the subject area embraces a particular area of human knowledge, (such as mathematics, physics, biology, social sciences, literature, foreign/second language, physical education).

2. Pedagogical competence requires knowledge of basic educational and psychological theories, methods, and practices; proficiency or skillfulness in teaching; and a caring attitude. Your approach to every student should stem from deeply held notions of fairness, honesty, and professional integrity.

● **FIGURE 12.1**

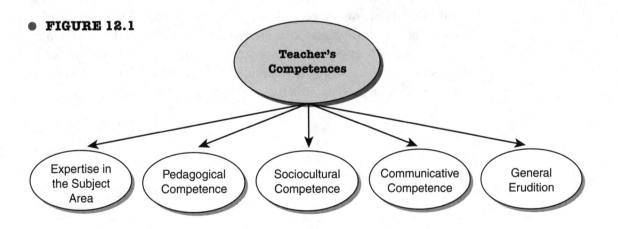

3. Sociocultural competence results in the ability to teach a diverse student population and be knowledgeable in community-based and service learning. In preparing a lesson plan, we should take into account various students' characteristics: their different intelligences and learning styles; their culture, ethnicity, race, previous education, life experiences, attitudes, and behaviors. The personal and scholastic rapport between teachers and their students emanating from a culturally responsive curriculum is critical for successful learning. This interaction has been called a "core relationship" of learning. Culturally sensitive approaches can build enduring teacher–learner relationships with students in a classroom ever more culturally and linguistically diverse.

4. Communicative competence allows a teacher to efficiently establish and develop communication with students and their parents, as well as with peers and colleagues. Instruction is essentially implemented through communication between the teacher and students. It should be well developed because it directly affects students' performance. This student-directed communication is not narrowed to content delivery only but includes feedback and exchange of messages during and beyond the class, in fact any type of verbal as well as non-verbal interaction. In short, education is in the conversation! Research indicates that the greater the parent involvement, generally the higher the student achievement. Furthermore, studies on parent involvement reveal that when a child's family is able to develop an environment that promotes learning, sets high expectations for achievement, and takes an active role in school and community, student success may be predicted with a high degree of confidence. This is why teacher–parent communication should be open, frequent, and continuous.

5. General erudition includes subjects that are essential for any educated professional, such as knowledge of history, literature, and other areas of universal knowledge. Students love and appreciate their teacher's expertise in any subject, cultural background, and experience. For example, American history may be one of your fortes, Russian music another, football a third.

● WHAT'S THE PLAN?

Which of these five teacher competences is your strongest?

_____

_____

_____

Which is your weakest?

_____

_____

Professional competence is commonly developed through years of study, teaching practice, life experiences, organized professional development, and self-directed lifelong learning. Again, overlaying all of these competences are the continual building and nurturing of personal moral standards and principles.

Methodological Concerns

We would like to stress here the importance of methodology that, as a part of pedagogy, is focused on practical issues of teaching and learning and on teaching particular subjects, such as ESL or mathematics. Methodology includes contemporary instructional approaches, strategies, techniques, and technologies. It also embraces lesson planning and content delivery, together with class organization and management.

Consequently, in methodology courses, lesson plan design and development as well as class organization and management need to be taught. Learning to write and implement a lesson plan is a very important part of a teacher's professional preparation. The teacher is actually a creator and a facilitator of learning goals, environments, activities, and outcomes.

Schools of education teach students of education a good deal of theory. What needs to be increased in teacher preparation is practical experience in all aspects of instruction, akin to what the students of engineering get in real-life problem-solving activities.

Practicing lesson plan design and development is as essential for teachers as is experimentation for physicists or chemists or learning to disassemble and assemble a car engine for an automobile mechanic.

Such an experience can be gained not only through teaching practice (field activities in school) but also through introducing lesson plan development in all methodology courses. This would have a positive effect on the outcome-based preparation of teacher candidates. The lesson plan is an indispensable instrument in teacher preparation.

Activities intended for lesson plan development may include: problem solving, analyzing different plans (found on the Web or presented on paper, in the video format, or in a class observation), designing lesson models, or developing fragments or full-blown plans and demonstrating them in front of a class (see Appendix D).

A very useful activity in teacher preparation is to ask a teacher candidate to videotape a lesson he or she teaches, then review the tape, reflect, and write a self-evaluation. The video can be watched in the college class and discussed with the peers and the instructor. Students generally believe it is one of the most efficient professional activities that give them an objective view of their performance.

The lesson plans teacher candidates write should be detailed and precise. Designing extensive lesson plans helps them develop the necessary skills for their future teaching experiences. This training could follow or be part of all methodology classes.

Teacher preparation in lesson plan development is, actually, a four-stage procedure:

1. *Analysis:* Examination of existing written lesson plans and of classroom teaching practice observations (live or videotaped)
2. *Synthesis:* New lesson plan design and development
3. *Application:* Demonstration of teaching according to the lesson plan
4. *Reflective assessment and evaluation:* Appraisal by you, a peer and an instructor

This procedure is shown in Figure 12.2.

This model of teacher preparation presupposes that the teacher previously acquired adequate theoretical knowledge necessary for plan development; it partially reflects Bloom's Taxonomy of Educational Objectives (1956). It allows a teacher candidate to develop strong lesson planning skills.

● **FIGURE 12.2**

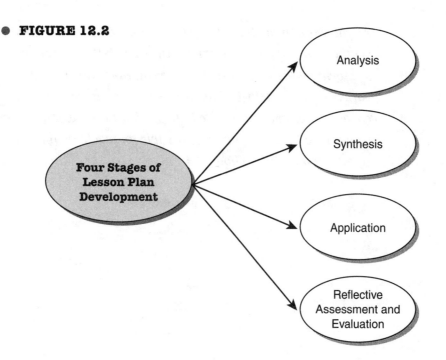

Practicing in lesson plan development is an objective in itself: It helps you to master organization, planning, and management of the instructional process; develops you as a professional; and prepares you for actual teaching.

● WHAT'S THE PLAN?

What lesson plan(s) do you plan on practicing? (***Hint:*** *By creating a video clip of your teaching, you can see yourself as others see you—assessing your own work as often as you wish whenever you wish!*)

_____

_____

_____

_____

_____

_____

_____

As you work through the four stages of lesson plan development: analyzing, synthesizing, applying, and reflecting, recall that lesson plans are aimed at providing the most enriched curriculum for all students via the widest variety of methodological approaches to set an environment where students choose to become self-directed lifelong learners. Lesson planning is and will continue to be the organizing principle for teaching and learning in the twenty-first century school.

APPENDIX A

···

Lesson Plan Development Guidelines for Students' Course Project

The methodological approach in second language development is a project-based activity with the goal of preparing students for actual teaching. Lesson plan development is the major part of understanding how to work successfully in this environment.

You may be asked to present a lesson plan as a package that will include both the detailed plan and teaching materials for the lesson. You may also need to demonstrate its implementation in the form of a virtual instruction in the class. Be sure to highlight you methodological approaches, strategies and techniques, especially SDAIE.

Lesson Plan Model
···

1. DESCRIPTION

Date: _____

Subject: _____

Topic: _____

Grade: _____

2. GOALS AND OBJECTIVES

Goals: _____

_____

_____

177

Objectives: _____
_____
_____

Standards: _____
_____

Accommodations for ELL/SDAIE: _____
_____
_____

Basic Vocabulary: _____
_____

3. MATERIALS AND TOOLS

Texts: _____
_____

Visuals: _____
_____

Technologies: _____
_____

Handouts: _____
_____

4. PROCEDURE

Introduction (_____ min.): _____
_____

Teacher Presentation (_____ min.): _____
_____

Class Activities (_____ min.): _____

_____

Homework (_____ min.): _____

_____

Closure (_____ min.): _____

_____

5. REFLECTIVE ASSESSMENT AND/OR EVALUATION

Conferences: _____

_____

Testing: _____

_____

Requirements

- Focus on the real instructional process and practical outcomes; try to see a class you are going to teach in your mind's eye.
- Describe lesson plan structure, procedures, and assignments, as well as evaluation, in detail.
- Supply teaching and learning materials.
- It is important to make research literature references.
- A video clip of a real lesson you taught would be a great plus.

Final Thoughts

Lesson content (what is to be taught), instructional procedures, including a focusing event (something to get the students' attention), teaching procedures (methods you will use), formative check (progress checks throughout the lesson); and student participation (how you will get the students to participate) can also be helpful.

APPENDIX B

Lesson Plan Development Assignments for Teacher Candidates

As lesson planning is an integral part of teacher preparation, it should be a major component of all methodology courses. The following are a few suggested assignments on lesson plan development that can be used in a methodology class:

1. Review several recommended literary sources on teaching ELL students (books, articles, teacher stories, online resources, and the like) and write an analytical survey with practical conclusions and recommendations as to what you will use in your practice and how you will use it.

2. From the Internet, select three lesson plans on one or similar topics intended for mainstream students. Use three different Web sites so that you can see various approaches. Analyze each of them and criticize them as regards goals, objectives, structure, instructional strategies, activities, technology applications, and assessment techniques. Note how ELL needs are addressed. Compare these three plans and find what is common to all. Suggest your improvements and write a short outline of your own lesson plan that will incorporate some of your findings.

3. Go on a virtual field experience. Find a "Best Practice" video presenting a lesson. Analyze and discuss the lesson structure, procedures, teacher's instructional style, and students' performance. Reflect and criticize the video, explain which instructional activities were efficient and which were not, point out to the mistakes, and offer ways to improve the lesson.

4. Visit three classes taught by three different teachers, observe the lessons; and analyze their plans and implementation, focusing on the teachers' performance, classroom management, and the students' cognitive and affective behavior. Check on the following: goals, objectives, outcomes, lesson structure, content

presentation, instructional strategies, learning activities, use of technology, student assessment, and class management techniques. Compare these lessons and your findings, then make conclusions. Offer constructive critique and suggestions for improvement.

5. Develop a lesson plan with a focus on structure, content, activities, and evaluation. Make necessary accommodations for a special education population. Present it on a paper as course work and demonstrate in class.

6. Demonstrate your lesson plan in your university class simulating teaching a 15- to 20-minute lesson (for the online class, video record your teaching this lesson in school or, if unavailable, to a group of age-appropriate students in your home). The use of at least one technology (PowerPoint, multimedia, video, or Web-based materials) is required. Based on your experiences, feedback from your peers and instructor (when applicable), and a review of your video clip (when applicable), write a self-evaluation paper on your lesson demonstration. Describe and critically assess your teaching experience. Reflect on the effectiveness of your lesson design and its implementation.

7. Analyze your peers' lesson plan presentations and write a critical observation paper.

8. Describe new material presentation in a lesson: Discuss all options, choose a few that will provide the best effect, describe methodology and techniques of presentation, and substantiate your strategies.

9. Compile a list of various activities for your content area, including subject, level, topic, and specific goals that you can implement in class.

10. Describe language input and activities in an ELL lesson: How can the teacher assist and facilitate students' second language development?

11. Analyze collaboration among students in lessons: Describe collaborative structures and strategies.

12. Analyze assessment and evaluation tools and methods.

13. Prepare a presentation for beginning teachers on lesson plan development. Highlight the most important items.

14. Write a research paper on current methodologies of ESL instruction that will help you select, evaluate, and implement methods of teaching and learning a second language.

15. Design a lesson plan in a content area of your choice that demonstrates second language development strategies. Consider implementing this lesson plan with ELL students.

16. You are participating in a panel at a teachers' conference. You are energetically supporting the SDAIE model, while your opponent is against it, criticizing various aspects of this model. Substantiate your point of view. This debate between two students can be conducted in class.

17. A school district has to make a decision: whether to accept the SDAIE model. There is a discussion among the board members; half are in support of SDAIE, and half are against. Each member of one team gives an argument for SDAIE, and each member of the opposite team offers an opposing point of view. The final decision will be taken in accordance with the team that has the most substantiated position. What is the most telling argument you could make for or against SDAIE?

18. Analyze your school/district's work on introducing and implementing the SDAIE model.

19. Use the 5-Star Lesson Plan to develop an approach for your own subject area and specific conditions, taking into account learning goals and objectives, level of your students, their entry level of proficiency in the subject, and sociocultural factors.

20. Watch an instructional video showing a "Best practices" lesson in school. Make up the plan of this lesson, describe the methods used, and offer your suggestions on how to improve the lesson structure and strategies.

21. Fill out the block scheme for the procedure component by appropriate units of activities (Figure B.1) (**Hint:** *Remember to include an introduction, presenting for better understanding and retention, accommodations for ELLs, class activities, homework, and closure.*)

● **FIGURE B.1**

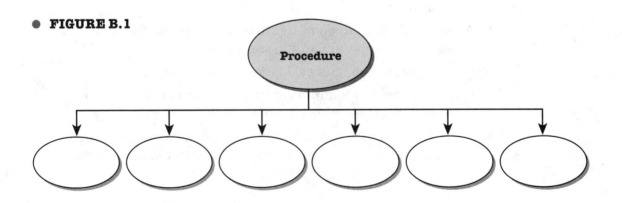

22. Fill out the block scheme for reflective assessment and evaluation module by appropriate units (Figure B.2). (**Hint:** *Remember student–teacher conferences, ongoing lesson assessment and revision, and testing.*)

● **FIGURE B.2**

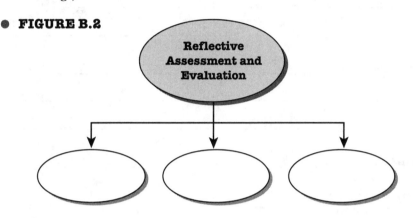

23. Fill out the block scheme for the 5-Star Lesson Plan by appropriate names of modules (Figure B.3).

● **FIGURE B.3**

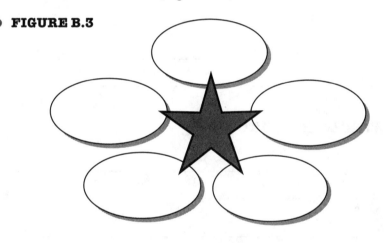

24. Fill out the following lesson plan model with appropriate information.

1. DESCRIPTION

Date: _____

Subject: _____

Topic: _____

Grade: _____

2. GOALS AND OBJECTIVES

Goals: _____

_____

_____

Objectives: _____

_____

_____

Standards: _____

_____

Accommodations for ELL/SDAIE: _____

_____

_____

Basic Vocabulary: _____

_____

3. MATERIALS AND TOOLS

Texts: _____

_____

Visuals: _____

_____

Technologies: _____

_____

Handouts: _____

_____

4. PROCEDURE

Introduction (_____ min.): _____

_____

Teacher Presentation (_____ min.): _____

_____

Class Activities (_____ min.): _____

_____

Homework (_____ min.): _____

_____

Closure (_____ min.): _____

_____

5. REFLECTIVE ASSESSMENT AND/OR EVALUATION

Conferences: _____

_____

Testing: _____

_____

25. Select and develop core subject content appropriate to ELLs' level of proficiency in listening, speaking, reading, and writing.

26. Apply appropriate strategies for developing and integrating the four language skills of listening, speaking, reading, and writing.

27. Identify, select, and apply appropriate instructional materials, tools, and technologies for ELLs in the content areas at elementary, middle, and high school levels.

28. Use formal and alternative methods of assessment and evaluation for ELLs, including measurement of language, literacy, academic content, and metacognition.

29. Develop and implement strategies for using school, community, and family resources in your content area and in ESL curricula.

APPENDIX C

Practice: Analyzing Lesson Plans

Below you will find four sample lesson plans developed to demonstrate the generic 5-Star Lesson Plan implementation, and a variety of activities that can be conducted in the classroom. These plans are united by a common theme, *The United States of America and its fifty states*, and one goal, *Enhance students' knowledge of the United States*. The lessons differ in topics and objectives. The topics are:

1. Basic geographical facts about the United States
2. Governing structures of the United States: The various states of the nation.
3. Basic facts about states; my own state
4. My home town

Each lesson has its own objectives that are intended to produce specific learning outcomes.

These four plans make up a unit. The information presented in the "Description" component of the first plan (subject, grade), in "Goals and objectives" (standards and accommodations) and in "Materials and tools" is the same for all the subsequent three lesson plans, so the details will be omitted there to avoid repetition.

Analyze these lesson plans, paying attention to how they are structured, what activities are used, and how students are guided to achieve the learning outcomes.

Lesson Plan 1

DESCRIPTION

Date: September 3, 200–

Subject: Geography

Topic: The United States of America and its fifty states: Basic geographical facts about the United States.

Grade: 5th (26 students, diverse class with 7 ELL students)

GOALS AND OBJECTIVES

Goal: Students will learn about the geography of the United States.

Objectives: Students will be able to:

1. Locate the United States on a map and describe its geography
2. Name the countries and oceans bordering the United States
3. Find the U.S. capital, Washington, DC on a map
4. Search, locate and use relevant information on the Internet
5. Demonstrate knowledge of basic facts about the country (territory, geographic zones, topography, climate and population) and be able to communicate it.

Standards: California History—Social Science Content Standard 3.1

Accommodations: Accommodations for students with special needs in this lesson may include the following adaptations to your methodological approach:

Adaptive Equipment:

- Ramps into and out of classroom
- Hand or foot controls
- Adjustable tables
- Enlarged texts
- Audio texts

In your teaching remember to:

- Explain lesson's vocabulary. Provide visual and other contextual clues when introducing new words.
- Repeat concepts when necessary.
- Create real-life situations for students to apply their new knowledge.
- Provide the necessary number of iterations of major concepts and skills for better retention. Sum up key points in the end of the lesson.
- Enhance learning via audiovisual aids.
- Use reflective assessments that can be done orally during and at end of lesson.

Your curriculum objectives and outcomes might be adapted or extended to meet specific student needs. You should have email and phone lists to seek assistance, if need be, from:

- Special educators
- Special education aides
- Paraprofessionals
- Interpreters
- Tutors
- Trained volunteers
- Your district office

Accommodations for ELL: Use the following support mechanisms when conducting specially designed academic instruction in English.

- Use a model: Organize learning material. Provide patterns and schemes. Select samples of what an acceptable answer to a question or finished product might look like (but try not to teach by ready-made samples). Recall that 80 percent of teaching is modeling.

- Engage via synthesis: Integrate a student's prior knowledge and build an analogy to construct a bridge of understanding to the student. Knowledge is associative, so seek connections with notions your students already possess.

- Help students to analyze new information to understand the underlying concepts and to make correct use of it.

- Employ metacognition: Teach your students to "think about how they think." Knowing one's learning style can help any student in the process of mastering new skills and knowledge.

- Connect via multisensory approaches: Use as many of the five senses as possible to present students with clues via sound, text, image and tactile experiences, and combine for students to effectively interact with knowledge and with other students.

Basic Vocabulary:

State	continent	ocean	river
country	North America	topography	lake
contiguous	territory	plain	climatic zone
land	border	mountain	capital
geography	coast		

▶ *Teaching Tip:* Presentation of this topic is conducted in four lessons and includes several instructional cycles: presentation of the new material by the teacher in each lesson, various classroom activities, such as small group work, discussions, a game of Snowball, a video with a subsequent discussion, questions to the class, homework, and finally singing a song. It is important to make the learning process for the whole topic connected, cohesive and complete (the principle of the whole and its parts).

MATERIALS AND TOOLS

Texts: Social Studies textbook

Web Links:

- States and capitals—http://www.50states.com/
- Yahoo! Get Local—http://dir.yahoo.com/Regional/U_S__States
- All 50 American States Global— http://www.globalcomputing.com/states.html
- Color Landform Atlas of the United States— http://fermi.jhuapl.edu/states/states.html
- Stately Knowledge: Facts about the United States— http://www.ipl.org/youth/stateknow/
- US States Crossword Puzzle—http://www.infoplease.com/states.html

Visuals: a map of the USA, a map of the state, city plan, United States Mats, U.S.A. Map Puzzle, Novel Notes *US Map*, travel books, albums, slides, National Geographic Journal, video *Travel Around the USA*, links to Web-based information about the United States, home state, and town.

Technologies: TV and DVD player or VCR, CD player or tape recorder, computer with Internet hookup, slide or LCD projector.

Handouts: lists of words, printouts of texts for reading, Lyrics of songs *The United States*, *States & Capitals*, *Rock'n Learn* from *National Geographic Journal*, useful information from the Internet.

PROCEDURE

Introduction (3 min.): Lately we have talked about the Earth, continents, oceans, and various countries. Today we will discuss the geography of the United States. Where is our country located, on which continent? What are the two oceans that wash its shores? What countries are our neighbors to the north and to the south? (These questions are directed at students to tap their prior knowledge.)

Teacher Presentation (15 min.): Today we are going to travel around our nation. We will see where it is situated, what countries and oceans border it, and how diverse it is. (The teacher makes an oral presentation of basic facts about the United States, specifically its geographic location, territory, relief, geographic zones, climate and population, finally talking about the capital. This presentation should be accompanied by various visuals: a big wall map, slides, photos, and video clips.)

Activities:

1. Now, ask me any questions about our country's geography: Where this country is located, what oceans its shores are washed by, which countries are our neighbors in the North and in the South, what are its major relief characteristics, and others. Every one of you can ask one question, and you cannot ask the same question twice. (6 min.).

2. Now we are going to break into groups and discuss the geography of the United States. You will have to prepare a report that will cover the following issues:
   - Natural borders
   - National borders
   - Major geographic features
   - Major climatic zones

   After you are done, one of you will present a short report from each group (6 min.)

3. Group presentations and discussion (12 min.)

REFLECTIVE ASSESSMENT AND EVALUATION (6 min.)

Students will be given a short oral test (see a sample below) and the answers will be assessed by their correctness:

What part of the world is the United States situated in?

What is the name of the ocean on its east coast?

What is the name of the ocean on its west coast?

What is the territory of the country in square miles?

Where is the capital of the United States located?

How many time zones are there in the United States?

▶ *Teacher Tips:*

1. Consider students' answers and comments

2. Keep a record of student participation

3. Note what questions students ask, who is going to the chalk board (front of the class) and showing the required items on the map; how active students are in activities, and who is presenting small group work to the whole class.

Homework (1 min.): In the textbook and on the Internet, please find three interesting facts about the United states, and in the next lesson share it with the class.

Closure (1 min.): Today we learned about the geographic situation of the United States, its territory, and time and climate zones. Geographic location of this nation determined many of the events in the past and will definitely play a role in the future. Knowing the geography of the place you live in may greatly help you in your life and future work. Do you have any questions?

Lesson Plan 2

DESCRIPTION

Date: September 4, 200–

Subject: Geography

Topic: The United States of America and its fifty states: Constituent units of the United States.

Grade: 5th (26 students, diverse class with 7 ELL students)

GOALS AND OBJECTIVES

Goals: Students will learn about different states and their geographical boundaries; remember the names of the fifty states and their capitals; know basic facts about the states.

Objectives: Students will be able to:

1. Define what a state is and how many make up the United States

2. Name the fifty states, their abbreviations, and their capitals

3. Find each of the states and their capitals on the map and describe their locations

4. Demonstrate knowledge of basic facts about the states (territory, geographic zones, topography, climate, and population) and be able to communicate it.

5. Improve writing and oral presentation skills

Standards: California History—Social Science Content Standard 3.1

Accommodations: Same

Basic Vocabulary: Names of the 50 states and their capitals, and the nation's capital; contiguous.

MATERIALS AND TOOLS

Same

PROCEDURE

Introduction (3 min.): Last time we talked about the United States geographic location, its topography and surrounding countries and oceans. Today we will look inside the country and see that it consists of smaller units called states. You may already know many of them. What is a state? (The students are expected to explain what a state is.)

Teacher Presentation (15 min.): A state is, as we learned, "one of the constituent units of a nation having a federal government" (Merriam-Webster Online Dictionary). The United States consists of fifty states that form the United States of America. (The teacher makes an oral presentation of basic facts about the fifty states, specifically their geographic locations and capitals. This presentation should be accompanied by various visuals: maps, slides, photos, and video clips.)

Activities:

1. Now let's play the Snowball game. One of you will give the name of one of the states. The second student will repeat this name and add another state. The third will repeat the first two names and add one more name. So it will go around the class until you add no new names. Don't repeat the same name. Understand? Let's play! (12 min.)

2. Probing students' knowledge (6 min.)
   You did a great job. How many states have we named? Do you know how many there are in all? So, how many more do we have to learn?

3. Revision (6 min.)
   Let's take a look at the map of the United States. As you can see, it is divided into many states.

   Q: Do you remember how many states there are?

   A: *Correct, fifty.*

   Q: What is a state?

   A: *Yes, a state is a part of the union, which has boundaries and makes laws that do not conflict the federal law.*

There are 48 contiguous states in the continental part of North America, and two states that are separated from the rest, Alaska, which is also in North America, and Hawaii in the Pacific Ocean.

Q: What can you say looking at the shape of the eastern states?

Λ:

Teacher: Yes, they have unusual shapes.

Q: Why, do you think this is so?

A:

Teacher: Right, rivers, lakes and mountains separate many of the states, and natural boundaries do not run in straight lines.

Q: Which is the largest state in territory?

A:

Teacher: Right Alaska

Q: And the largest in population?

A:

Teacher: Right, California

Q: Which is the smallest state in territory?

A:

Teacher: Rhode Island

Q: And the smallest in population?

Teacher: Yes, Wyoming

Q. Do you know how many original states there were?

A: *Right, 13.*

Q: Do you know each state has a two-letter abbreviation? What is short for California, for example?

A:

Teacher: Yes, CA

The revision is conducted in the form of the questions and answers with teacher corrections and prompts as well as short narratives inserted when necessary to expand new knowledge. The teacher relates the information accompanying the story by pointing to the states on the map.

4. Small group (three student teams) work (7 min.). A puzzle game: in a group of three, put together the map of the country using a puzzle map of the United States.

ASSESSMENT AND EVALUATION (4 min.)

The teacher assesses students' understanding and knowledge by asking questions, such as:

- So, how many states are there in the United States?
- Which is the largest state in territory?

- Which is the largest state in population?
- Which is the smallest state in territory?
- Which is the smallest state in population?

▶ *Teacher Tips:*

1. Consider students' answers and comments
2. Keep a record of student participation
3. Note what questions students ask, who is going to the board (front of the class) and showing the states on the map; how active students are in activities, and who is presenting small group work to the whole class.

Homework (1 min.): At home you will prepare a short story. Write about any state except our own. Include all the basic facts about your state, including its location, capital, territory, topography, climate, population, and major highlights. You can use both the textbook and the Internet to find these facts. Bring the stories to the class next time to share with us.

Closure (2 min.): Today we learned major facts about the United States. There are big states and small states, the topography of some of them integrates ocean coasts, mountains, forests, and/or deserts. Each of the states has its own characteristics, such as location, natural resources, and landmarks. Some day you may move to another state, and this information will be helpful to you. Any questions?

Lesson Plan 3

DESCRIPTION

Date: September 5, 200–

Subject: Geography

Topic: The United States and its fifty states: Basic facts about states; my own state

Grade: 5th (26 students, diverse class with 7 ELL students)

GOALS AND OBJECTIVES

Goals: Students will learn basic geographical facts about their home state.

Objectives: Students will be able to:

1. Search, locate, select, and evaluate relevant information on the Internet
2. Discuss major facts about the United States
3. Describe their home state
4. Demonstrate knowledge of basic facts about their home state: geographic location, neighboring states, capital, climate, population, major landmarks, and use those facts in oral and written communication

Standards: California History—Social Science Content Standard 3.1

Accommodations: Same

Basic Vocabulary:

home state	territory	landmark
contiguous	topography	resource
neighboring state	climate	industry
state capital	population	business

MATERIALS AND TOOLS

Same

PROCEDURE

Introduction (**4 min.**): We have learned about our country and its states. (The teacher will briefly review the previous lesson.) Today we are going to continue our travel around the United States and then we will talk about our home state. The teacher can start the new topic by asking students the following questions:

- What state do we live in?
- What is the capital of our state?
- What are the neighboring states?
- Where are they located? Show on the map.
- What states have you been to?
- Do you know how many states there are?
- What is the capital of the United States?

Presentation (**12 min.**): The teacher offers a video demonstration: Now you are going to travel around our country and watch a short video, *Around the United States,* to see what we have talked about recently. You will recognize the states and their names. Make a mental note of at least one specific characteristic of each of the states. After the video we will share our notes and impressions in the discussion.

Activities:

1. Small group (4 students each) discussion. Now, after we made a tour of our country, let's see what impressed you most. I'd like everybody to say a few words about the most interesting part of the video. Share your observations, discuss them, and make up a list of five major facts that you will present to the class. (6 min.)
2. Class discussion of the findings (8 min.)
3. Singing the Song (7 min.).

There have been quite a few songs composed about this country. Let's hear one of them, which provides information about the states and their capitals. Then you will get the lyrics and we will sing it together. Later you will learn this song by memory.

▶ *Teaching Tips:* A fun way to learn the states and capitals of the United States is by singing songs. One resource which includes lyrics and recorded music is called *States & Capitals: Rock'n Learn.* The first song lists the states in alphabetic order followed by their capitals. Students listen, rap along, and follow the lyrics in the book. Two other songs can be used by the teacher if and when it is appropriate, according to the plan. The second song presents the states and their capitals in a mixed-up order. A longer delay allows more time for a student to sing along with the voice on tape. The third song gives practice naming the states in each geographic region.

Second presentation (5 min.): The teacher presents a short overview of the home state's major characteristics using a map and visuals. Local artifacts, such as minerals found in the state, items manufactured in the state, pictures of state landmarks will be useful.

After this presentation, the teacher asks questions to identify what students know about the state. (5 min.)

Homework (2 min.):

- Make up a list of the most important state landmarks you know.
- Find out 10 important facts about one of the states (The states are distributed among students). Use the books in the school library and the Internet.
- Interview your parents about one of the states they have visited and write their story to read in class.
- Learn to sing the song about the US states and capitals.

▶ *Teaching Tip:* Homework can be given to students on individual pieces of paper.

Closure (1 min.): Today we learned more about the United States. Now we know the names and capitals of the fifty states. We also know where they are located and can find them on the map. Some day you may wish to take a vacation in a state you have described for our class. When you travel you will recognize some of the things we learned today. Next time we will learn more about our home state and town.

REFLECTIVE ASSESSMENT AND EVALUATION

- Consider students' answers and comments
- Keep a record of student participation
- Note who is going to the board (front of the class) and showing the states on the map.

Conferences: Meet with students on an on-going basis to converse about their comprehension (e.g. Before we finish our lesson, I will ask one of you to come up and tell me what we have learned today about the 50 states, showing them on the map.)

Lesson Plan 4

DESCRIPTION

Date: September 6, 200–

Subject: Geography

Topic: The United States of America and its fifty states: my home town

Grade: 5th (26 students, diverse class with 7 ELL students)

GOALS AND OBJECTIVES

Goals: Enhance students' knowledge of their home town, its geography, environment, and industries bases on local resources to increase their awareness of where they live.

Objectives: Students will be able to:

1. Describe their home town and its geography
2. Demonstrate knowledge of basic facts about the town: topography, climate, environment, industries, and population
3. Improve their reading, writing, and oral presentation skills

Vocabulary:

home town	climate	resource
topography	population	industries
territory	landmark	business
environment	place of interest	

Standards: California History—Social Science Content Standard 3.1

Accommodations: Same.

MATERIALS AND TOOLS

Same.

PROCEDURE

Introduction (3 min.): Lately we have learned about the country and its fifty states, including our own home state. (The teacher will briefly review the previous lesson.) Today our main topic will be our home town, its geography, topography, environment, resources, major industries and businesses, landmarks, and places of interest. It will be more interesting to live in the town when we learn all the facts about it, won't it?

Presentation (5 min.): The teacher will ask two students who had previously been given individual assignments to make a presentation on the town, describing its geographic characteristics. Presentations will be illustrated by visuals (pictures, slides and, if available, a video clip).

Activities:

1. In groups of three, make up a list of the town's major landmarks and places of interest, and then present your findings to the class. (8 min.)

2. We will have 6 groups in class, each group representing a different travel company in town. As different towns have many places of natural beauty, landmarks, and historical sites, each company wishes to attract more tourists from all over the country as well as from overseas to enjoy the scenic and educational wonders of the town and state. The task will be to develop plans of how to attract more tourists to the states. A part of the project will be to write an advertisement that would describe the town in the most attractive way. So, develop a plan and write this ad. Then present it to the class. (15 min.)

Homework (3 min.):

1. Class project: Let's write a class book *The States of the Union* with pictures. We will distribute states among you, and each of you will write a description about one state. This report will have to tell us about its location, capital, landmarks, industry, state nickname, state bird and state animal, what grows and what is found underground. Find three pictures about your state and attach them to your report. Use the books in the school library, *National Geographic,* and Internet resources. After we collect all your reports, we will compile them into the book, which we all can share. This project will have to be completed in two weeks. Write a report on the chosen state for the project.

2. Send an electronic postcard to one of your class mates using the *1001 Postcards web site.*

Closure (1 min.): Today we learned more about our own town. Someday you may be hosting a member of your family from another place, or a friend from far away, and you will be able to make an interesting sightseeing tour of the town. In addition, we began a class project, *The States of the Union,* in which we all will share information about our nation. This project will conclude the topic *The United States of America and its fifty states.*

REFLECTIVE ASSESSMENT AND EVALUATION

A Written Test (15 min.)

Part 1. Matching (25 points): Present students with two columns of 10 different states (in the right hand column) and their capitals (in the left hand column). Match the state with the capital by drawing a line from one to the other.

Part 2. Short Essay (75 points): Based on your new knowledge, explain, in about 100 words, which state would you like to visit and why?

The test will be collected and graded by the next lesson.

APPENDIX D

Sample Lesson Plans

Lesson Plan 1

LESSON DESCRIPTION

Content Area: Language Arts

Title: Vocabulary Building

Grade Level: 1–3 (primary)

Author: Adapted from: Judy Ezell, Fort Gibson Elementary, Fort Gibson, OK

Rationale: Elementary students tend to use a limited vocabulary. Teachers can introduce new words in ways that are fun and enriching. There are various activities that offer opportunities for children to brainstorm lists of words to be used in sentences, stories, or conversation.

GOALS

The goal of the lesson is to help students increase their vocabulary for use in a given situation.

OBJECTIVES

As a result of these activities, students will be able to:

- *Meet standards:* Classify grade-appropriate categories of words (such as plants, animals, foods, toys, classroom objects) by
  1. Relating situations to specific word groups
  2. Using new words in reading, writing and speaking on the topic
  3. Employing a web to collect ideas

MATERIALS AND TOOLS

- Supply of magazines
- Paper to make fruit or letter shapes
- A variety of story books
- Pictures illustrating new words and their use
- A video clip on the topic
- A DVD player and TV

ELL Adaptation: The teacher writes on the chalkboard or shows a poster with words describing several different categories and explains their meaning (separately for each category). Pictures illustrating these words can be helpful. The teacher reads each word aloud and asks students to repeat them in chorus. Students may write their first language equivalents together with new words in their vocabulary list or notebook.

PROCEDURES

Introduction (4 min.): Students will be told and shown images about grade-appropriate vocabulary and ways to build it. Previous activities will be reviewed. Several new collective activities will be useful for developing vocabulary, such as cooperative learning, brainstorming, and webbing. These activities can be used at any time and for any subject.

Presentation (10 min.): Teacher explains these activities:

Cooperative learning: Begin with the large group and teach students to accept each other's ideas (no put-downs); everyone can take a risk and be accepted. As the students learn to work in groups, set up small groups to collect ideas.

Brainstorming: Allow each student to give you a word related to a color, a theme (such as bears, whales, or a season), or a feeling (such as sad, happy, excited, or upset). Guide these discussions in an accepting manner and encourage everyone to participate.

Webbing, mapping, and, according to Nancy Margulies, author of Mapping Inner Space, *Mind Mapping:* Draw a picture of your subject or place the word in the center of your board or paper. Connect words or pictures related to your main subject with radiating lines from the central picture or word. When words are written (under the pictures), hang these papers up for children to use as word banks.

Activities (30 min.):

1. Read a nursery rhyme and have children think of other words to fit in place of a selected word that mean the same thing (synonym) or expand and mean the opposite (antonym). Divide students in small groups of four and let them work in groups. A representative from each group will present their finding to the whole class.

2. Using a large fruit shape, write the other things the children name that are the same color. Use a brainstorming technique.

3. Using a large letter shape, have children cut out pictures of things that begin with that letter. Do this activity in small groups of three, emphasizing the importance of cooperation.

4. Write the name of a book just read in the middle of the board. Have students tell about the characters, setting, problem, and conclusion as you "map" their ideas in words or pictures using a webbing technique.

5. Using a theme—such as Thanksgiving, summer vacation, the zoo, or the sun—write all the words or collect pictures related to the theme. For individual work, have the whole class read the words in turn, using only new words that have not yet been read.

6. Show the video clip on the topic to students and ask to discuss what they saw using the new vocabulary.

REFLECTIVE ASSESSMENT AND EVALUATION

Student performance will be assessed continuously by observing their individual and group work and their presentations. Necessary corrections will be made in the process of the lesson individually by affirming effort and repeating correct pronunciation and usage. Typical errors will be addressed before the whole class during closure.

Homework (3 min.): After you have divided students into pairs, they will be given an assignment to write a list of words related to going on vacation with a friend and communicating over the telephone. Suggest that students use the computer and the Internet at home or in the school lab or library to search for topic-related situations. This assignment will be presented by different combinations of pairs of students in the next lesson. Parents will be notified about helping their children practice this assignment at home.

Closure (3 min.): The teacher will review today's work, highlighting major points such as new words and new collaborative techniques and praising students' effort.

Lesson Plan 2

LESSON DESCRIPTION

Content Area: Math

Title: Block It

Grade Level: Grades 1–3 (primary)

Author: Adapted from: Fay Zenigami, Leeward District Office, Waipahu, Hawaii.

Rationale: Students in primary grades need varied activities to help them learn basic facts about mathematical operations.

GOALS

The goal of the lesson is to reinforce computational skills using this problem solving game based on pattern blocks.

OBJECTIVES

As a result of these activities students will be able to:
- *Meet standards:* Students use computation skills and problem-solving strategies that involve geometric shapes and patterns by
  1. Applying problem solving strategies such as guess and check and visualization to play the game
  2. Using mental mathematics to decide on the placement of pattern blocks
  3. Finding patterns for effective problem solving

MATERIALS AND TOOLS

- Pattern blocks
- Paper on which to keep score
- Calculator

ELL Adaptation: The teacher writes on the chalkboard or shows a poster with words denoting math operations and explains their meaning. The teacher reads each word aloud and asks students repeat them in chorus. Students may write their first-language equivalents together with new words in their vocabulary list or notebook.

PROCEDURES

Introduction (5 min.): Students will be reminded about math operations. Previous activities will be reviewed. Several new collective activities will be useful for developing vocabulary, such as cooperative learning, brainstorming, and webbing. These activities can be used at any time and for any subject.

Presentation (8 min.): The teacher explains problem-solving strategies such as guess and check and visualization. Students will be told about mental mathematics and pattern blocks.

Activities (32 min.):

1. Two players are needed to play "Block It." So, the class will be divided in pairs. Each player receives three of the following pattern blocks: green triangle, blue rhombus, red trapezoid, yellow hexagon.
2. Players agree on assigned points for each color (for example, green = 1, blue = 2, red = 3, yellow = 6).
3. The game begins with one yellow hexagon starting block placed on the playing surface. This piece does not belong to either player. The first player must place one of her or his blocks such that one side of the block is completely touching on one side of the block(s) on the playing surface. The scoring for each play is the sum of the values of the block placed and those that it touches on a side. Play continues until both players use all of their pieces.

   For example, Player A selects a green triangle to play, therefore the green triangle (1 point) touches the yellow hexagon (6 points) so 7 points (1 + 6) are scored. Player B then places a red trapezoid (3 points) such that it touches one full side of the green triangle (1 point) and one full side of the yellow hexagon (6 points); Player B scores 10 points (3 + 1 + 6). Player A places a blue rhombus (2 points) that touches one full side of the green triangle (1 point) and one full side of the yellow hexagon (6 points), which scores another 9 points (2 + 1 + 6) giving Player A a total now of 16 points. Player B continues play in this manner.
4. Students may use a calculator to help them keep score.
5. The player with the most total points after all pieces have been used is the winner.

REFLECTIVE ASSESSMENT AND EVALUATION

Students will be assessed based on the following questions:

1. Have students shared their scores and strategies?
2. What were the most and fewest points a player scored in one play in your game?
3. Did students use the blocks with higher point values first or last?
4. Does Player A have an advantage by going first?
5. Is there a maximum score a player can earn?
6. If the pieces were assigned different values, how would that affect their play?

Homework (2 min.): Students will be given two problems to solve. Parents will be notified about monitoring their children to see the assignment is completed.

Closure (3 min.): The teacher will review the lesson's main points.

Lesson Plan 3

LESSON DESCRIPTION

Content Area: Science

Title: Animals

Grade Level: K–3 (primary)

Author: Adapted from: Sandra J. Rost, Lewis-Arriola Elementary School Cortez, Colorado

Rationale: Students report finding the study of science "boring and difficult." They do not seem to have a working knowledge of how to go about posing scientific questions and finding answers in the real world around them.

GOAL

This lesson will help students become familiar with the need for categorizing scientific information, in this case, animals.

OBJECTIVES

As a result of these activities, students will be able to:

- *Meet standards:* Observe and describe similarities and differences in the appearance and behavior of selected animals by
    1. Categorizing the five groups of animals (mammals, fish, birds, reptiles, and amphibians)
    2. Describing each of them

MATERIALS AND TOOLS

- DVDs, films, filmstrips, or slides about animals (must include all five categories of animals)
- Live or mounted animals from each category (State Division of Wildlife Agency and public zoos may be able to help you find these)
- Magazines: Two per child (make sure the magazines have plenty of animal pictures in them)
- Scissors

ELL Adaptation: The teacher writes on the chalkboard or shows a poster with words describing animals and explains their meaning. Pictures illustrating these words are necessary. The teacher reads each word aloud and asks students repeat them in chorus. Students may write their first language equivalents together with new words in their vocabulary list or notebook.

PROCEDURES

Introduction (6 min.): Students will be asked to tell about the animals they know, including their pets. Previous activities will be reviewed.

Presentation (6 min.): The teacher describes various groups of animals.

Activities (33 min.):

1. (5 min.) Discuss with students the process of separating animals into groups or categories so that they are more easily studied and discussed by scientists and others. Explain that the following activity will help students learn about the categories of animals. Do not give any clues at this time as to how animals are to be categorized. Students will come up with their own unique system of grouping.

2. (8 min.) Divide students into small groups of three to five. Give each child one or two magazines that have a lot of animal pictures (such as *National Geographic, Outdoors, Field and Stream*). Students in each group look through the magazines and cut out any pictures of animals that they find. Have students keep a common stack for their group.

3. (5 min.) After all pictures have been put into a pile, each group divides their pile of pictures into five to seven smaller categories. This is done through small group discussion and consensus.

4. (6 min.) After each group has categorized their pictures, bring the entire class back together and let one person from each group explain why they grouped their pictures as they did. (They may come up with groupings by color, size, shape, whether the animal is extinct or not, eating habits, living habits, size of ears and/or tails, and the like. They will come up with categories you and I would never dream of!)

5. (9 min.) Show a DVD or film to the class about the actual categories into which scientists have divided animals. Discuss these groups and why it helps scientists to have animals broken down into smaller groups. Show students live or mounted animals. (Mounted samples are often available through state wildlife agencies.) Have students bring in pets that fit the various categories and discuss them.

REFLECTIVE ASSESSMENT AND EVALUATION

Observe students' individual and group activities. Notice their errors and try to help them find the right solution. Approach and advise individual students as you are complimenting them for their effort.

Homework (2 min.): Depending on the age of the student, ask for

1. A picture book of ten or more animals with category names on each page (may be constructed from magazine pictures or the child's drawings).

2. An essay about their favorite animal using available literature and multimedia information.

Parents will be asked to monitor this assignment at home.

Closure (3 min.): Suggest that one or two students review the lesson, mentioning all five categories and their major characteristics.

Lesson Plan 4

LESSON DESCRIPTION

Content Area: Social Studies

Title: Community Helpers

Grade Level: K–2 (primary)

Author: Adapted from: Shirley Sutton, Parkside Elementary, Powell, Wyoming

Rationale: Many children see community helpers only as those people who wear uniforms or have jobs that we see or hear about on television. The children often do not realize there are many other workers who contribute to a successful community.

GOALS

The goal of this lesson is to help the children realize that it takes many varied jobs for a city or town to work as a community and to teach them ways to do their share in helping their community.

OBJECTIVES

As a result of these activities, students will be able to:

- *Meet standards:* Discuss the importance of work and the role of citizens, including how to become involved in the community as well as in the classroom.

  1. List and describe many varied and unusual jobs that people might have in the community

2. Identify the purpose of the work done by their parents either in the home or outside of the home

3. Suggest different ideas for their participation in the community

4. Involve parents in a school learning activity

MATERIALS AND TOOLS

- A note home (explaining the project and asking for parental assistance), chart paper, marker, adult helpers to write stories
- Student materials: Paper, pencil, crayons

ELL Adaptation: The teacher writes on the chalkboard or shows a poster with words describing community activities and explains their meaning. The teacher reads each word aloud and asks students to repeat them in chorus. Students may write their first-language equivalents together with new words in their vocabulary list or notebook.

PROCEDURES

Introduction (6 min.): Students will be asked to tell about their personal experiences with their community involvement. Various community service activities will be discussed.

Presentation (4 min.): The teacher explains the role and benefits of community involvement, public service, and the student's role in the classroom.

Activities (32 min.):

1. Divide students into small groups of three to five. Ask them to make a list of the jobs people might have.

2. Bring in the "tools of the trade" of one or both of their parents. The child should be able to explain the tool as a part of their parent's work. (examples: wrench, computer paper, measuring spoon, disposable diaper)

3. Parents may come in to demonstrate their "tools of the trade."

4. Students will draw and write (or dictate) a story about a person using their parents' tools.

5. Students will draw and tell about what they might like to do when they grow up and how their work in the classroom will help them get to where they want to go in life.

6. Again divide students into small groups of three to five. Ask them to identify the needs of the community and offer their participation in solving the problems. Discuss every student's possible contribution to the community.

7. Take a field trip next time to observe the jobs performed by the various helpers.

REFLECTIVE ASSESSMENT AND EVALUATION

1. Check by asking questions how students understood community needs and community helpers jobs.

2. Discuss how listening, speaking, reading, and writing in the classroom can help a student prepare for the future.

3. Share their stories with their classmates and families.

Homework (2 min.): Ask students to perform an age appropriate activity:

1. Draw a picture about a person they know and the kind of job that person does

2. Write an essay about a person they know or met, including a family member, who does community service

Parents will be asked to provide "tools of the trade" and monitor the successful completion of this homework assignment.

Closure (6 min.): Suggest that students discuss jobs that help their community.

Lesson Plan 5

LESSON DESCRIPTION

Content Area: Art

Title: They Put On Masks

Grade Level: K–8 (elementary to intermediate)

Author: Adapted from: Darlene Prina, Arapahoe School, Fremont City, Wyoming

Rationale: Mask making is an activity that can develop higher-order thinking skills. It also helps disseminate the knowledge of art history. Students learn the ritual and the technique of mask making from several cultures besides their own. Students will be engaged in cooperative learning activities.

GOALS

Students will develop a greater perspective of other traditions and beliefs. They will gain experience in exploring several media forms. Students also will learn to work together, to share and care.

OBJECTIVES

As a result of these activities, student will be able to:

- *Meet standards:* Describe works of art that are used versus those that are only viewed; recognize and describe works of art that show people doing things together; and discuss works of art from other cultures by

  1. Cooperating with each other in solving real-life problems

  2. Learning to manipulate a variety of media

3. Exploring traditions of several cultures and being able to describe them

4. Developing new, creative ways to appreciate art

5. Cultivating their understanding of self-worth

MATERIALS AND TOOLS

- Slides of Native American art
- Literature on African or any other culture that celebrates with masks
- Plaster of paris
- Paris craft plaster strips, buckets, and warm water
- Rafia acrylic paint, brushes, glass medium
- Sculpty mold compound
- Beans and peas
- Scissors, paper, markers, Vaseline, pantyhose
- Drop cloths and plastic
- An expert or mask-making artist in nearby area can invited to the class

ELL Adaptation: The teacher asks students to write on the chalkboard new words and then invites the class to explain their meaning. The teacher reads each word aloud and asks students repeat them in chorus. Students may write their first-language equivalents together with new words in their vocabulary list or notebook.

PROCEDURES

Introduction (5 min.): The teacher explains what folk art is. Then students will be asked to tell about their personal knowledge and experience with folk art.

Presentation (15 min.): The teacher explains various arts, demonstrating with slides and video clips.

Activities (26 min.):

1. View and discuss a slide presentation of Native American art.

2. Explore African mask-making, viewing pictures.

3. Attend a demonstration by community mask-maker, viewing a variety of masks made nationally and usage of masks in ceremonies (before the lesson).

4. In groups of four:
   - Create a picture draft of the mask.

   The following can be accomplished in subsequent lessons:
   - Prepare for making masks.
   - Make masks.
   - Decorate masks.
   - Present your mask to the class, explaining your idea behind it.

5. Create a skit for the school to view.

6. Display the masks.

REFLECTIVE ASSESSMENT AND EVALUATION

Students display masks with a "special" name together with stories of their purpose or create a skit for other selected classes to observe, after which the masks are displayed. Then the students self-assess, using the following questions: What design principles and elements have I used? What do I especially like, and what will I do differently next time? Then students act together as judges at an exhibition, discussing the merits and flaws of each mask and assigning points to them, eventually selecting a winner.

Homework (1 min.): Consider age appropriate homework

1. Construct a sketch of the mask to be made in class.

2. Write an essay about a piece of art of your choice.

Parents should monitor work as the student explains the assignment to them.

Closure (3 min.): Sum up the lesson, identifying major trends in art, and have a discussion about how masks from different cultures enrich everyone's appreciation of art.

Lesson Plan 6

LESSON DESCRIPTION

Content Area: Interdisciplinary (language arts, science, and social studies)

Title: Knowing ourselves and each other through poetry

Grade Level: 6–12 (middle school to high school)

Author: Adapted from: Missy Kasbaum, Cushing, OK

Rationale: Developing a rapport and trust with students at risk of dropping out of school is often difficult. These students are guarded in their openness with adults in general and school staff in particular. Yet providing an open atmosphere is fundamental to mending self-concepts and a prerequisite for skill development and the academic success necessary leading to graduation.

GOALS

The goal for this lesson is getting to know students and getting them to know themselves through writing.

OBJECTIVES

As a result of these activities, students will be able to:

- *Meet standards:* Understand how meaning is essential to poetry via the marriage of sound and sense through word choice, figurative language, line structure, line length, punctuation, rhythm, repetition, and rhyme;

identify and analyze features of themes and concomitant emotions conveyed through characters, actions, and images; plus explain the effects of common literary devices (such as symbolism, imagery, and metaphor) in poetry by

1. Becoming more familiar with word usage and learning to use synonyms

2. Identifying and describing the degrees(s) of emotion contained in words and explaining the use of language to express meaning and emotions

MATERIALS AND TOOLS

- Ferguson/Florisant Writing Project, which is part of the National Diffusion Network offerings found in the EPTW (Educational Programs That Work) Directory
- Selected works of poetry

ELL Adaptation: The teacher writes on the chalkboard or shows a poster with words and images denoting emotions and explains their meaning. Pictures illustrating emotions can be helpful. Students may write their first-language equivalents together with new words in their vocabulary list or notebook.

PROCEDURES

Introduction (6 min.): Students will be asked to tell about feelings and emotions. Then have each student write down a word that describes how he or she feels today.

Use this model: Today I feel (*emotion*) because (*give reason*).

Presentation (6 min.): The teacher will explain what feelings and emotions are. Interestingly, it is possible to have more than one emotion or feeling during the same day, either similar or opposite. This presentation can be illustrated by various pictures, slides, and video clips.

Activities (33 min.):

1. Begin a discussion of what feelings and emotions are. Examples: Today I feel worried because we are having a test. Also, I feel happy because today is Friday. To help students examine emotions more closely, use this exercise: After brainstorming a list of emotions, ask students to choose one and assign it a color. "Pride is purple," or "Happiness is yellow." Use the following to further explore:

(*Emotion*) is (*Color*).	Fear is red.
It smells like _____.	It smells like fire.
It tastes like _____.	It tastes like rotten peaches.
It sounds like _____.	It sounds like car horns.
It feels like _____.	It feels like sand paper.
It looks like _____.	It looks like Freddy Krueger.
(*Emotion*) is (*Give a metaphoric statement*).	Fear is falling into a hole.

2. Teach students to write "Bio-poems":

Line 1	Your first name only
Line 2	Four traits that describe you
Line 3	Sibling of . . . (or son/daughter of)
Line 4	Lover of . . . (three people or ideas)
Line 5	Who feels . . . (three items)
Line 6	Who needs . . . (three items)
Line 7	Who gives . . . (three items)
Line 8	Who fears . . . (three items)
Line 9	Who would like to see . . . (three items)
Line 10	Resident of (your city, street or state)
Line 11	Your last name only

Example:
Kaitlan
Petite, bubbly, happy and energetic.
Daughter of Greg and Missy
Lover of gymnastics, roses, and cheerleading
Who feels happiness with friends, loneliness at night, and joy at ball
    games
Who needs friends, love, and acceptance
Who gives friendship, love, and encouragement
Who fears pain, death, and losing friends
Who would like to see the world, the future, and never ending joy
Resident of Stigler, Oklahoma
Kasbaum

In content areas, students can synthesize key concepts or characters to extract meaning and gain understanding. This exercise can be used for analysis of literary characters. Historical events and characters work well, as do the characteristics of animals, plants, or chemical elements, with variations in lines 3 through 9 to suit the subject.

3. Divide the class in groups of four and ask each group to identify creative and destructive emotions. Then ask each group to present their findings to the class.

REFLECTIVE ASSESSMENT AND EVALUATION

Students will be assessed on the performance and evaluated on assignment completion.

Homework (2 min.): Ask students to write a poem about their feelings. Suggest the efficacy and art of free verse. Parents can monitor to see the work is completed.

Closure (3 min.): Ask students to sum up the lesson describing major feelings and emotions and explaining the role emotions play in our life and how they can be expressed poetically. It would be useful to help students understand ways to cope with emotions.

Lesson Plan 7

LESSON DESCRIPTION

Content Area: Math

Title: Smile Metric Style

Grade Level: 4–8 (intermediate)

Author: Adapted from: Deana Metzler

Rationale: Using the metric system can be very confusing and difficult for many students. This lesson enables the students to practice working with the metric system.

GOALS

The goal of this lesson is to help students understand and apply the metric system.

OBJECTIVES

As a result of these activities, students will be able to:

- *Meet standards:* Demonstrate an understanding of different units of measure and the ability to use the metric system for measurements by
    1. Using a metric ruler to accurately measure length
    2. Reading and recording accurate measurements taken in centimeters and millimeters
    3. Finding a sum of multiple metric measurements
    4. Comparing and ordering individual measurements
    5. Using a histogram to graph their results

MATERIALS AND TOOLS

- Metric ruler
- Crayons or markers
- Pencils
- Paper
- Chalkboard
- Chalk
- Large piece of construction paper or butcher paper
- Graph paper

ELL Adaptation: The teacher writes on the chalkboard or shows a poster with words denoting metric units and explains their meaning. The teacher reads each word aloud and asks students to repeat them in chorus. Students may write their first-language equivalents together with new words in their vocabulary list or notebook.

PROCEDURES

Introduction (4 min.): Students will be asked to discuss various measurement systems they know.

Presentation (6 min.): The teacher will explain two major measurement systems, traditional and metric ones. A table comparing different measurements will be useful.

Activities (28 min.):

1. Divide the class into groups of four. Each student will measure and record the length of each person's smile in their group. The students need to check their results against the results of the rest of the group. If there are any discrepancies, the students should verify the results as a group. When an accurate measurement has been obtained for each child, the results are recorded on the chalkboard as each child records them at his or her seat. Order all the measurements from least to greatest. Graph your results. Find the sum of all the smiles in your classroom. Don't forget the teacher's; he or she often has the largest smile because the students are so involved in this activity.

2. Create one smile out of construction paper that is the length of all the smiles in your room.

3. Offer students to individually measure different objects and report their findings to the class.

This lesson can be completed as one lesson or extended to several, depending on the level and ability of the class. A fun extension to this activity is to challenge other classes to measure their smiles and gather data. These data can then be compiled and totaled by each class. A graph is then constructed comparing individual classes and posted in the main hall. The graph generates a lot of interest and sets an environment where students choose to be motivated to measure and compare many other objects.

REFLECTIVE ASSESSMENT AND EVALUATION

Students will be assessed on their accuracy of measurements and presentations to the class. A quiz can be offered after the activities (7 min.).

Homework (2 min.): Ask students to measure three objects in their house. Students can explain to their parents different units of measurement, and parents can monitor the learning activity.

Closure (3 min.): Overview the lesson and measurement systems and summarize students' activities. Explain the practical importance of measurements.

Lesson Plan 8

LESSON DESCRIPTION

Content Area: Science

Title: Photosynthesis and Transpiration

Grade Level: 6–8 (intermediate)

Author: Adapted from: Nelida Boreale, Mountain View Elementary, Arizona

Rationale: Many students are not interested in science at all. They often think that the concepts taught in science are irrelevant to their needs. They believe that science is boring and hard to understand. Until children experience science in a fun way with a spirit of discovery, their attitude toward science won't change. This lesson is to be conducted in three steps: An assignment should be given to students a few days before the lesson, then the lesson will be taught, after the lesson it will take about ten days to conduct the experiment and then report to the class.

GOALS

The goal is to help students experience science in a different way. This will help change students' negative attitudes toward science into positive ones.

OBJECTIVES

As a result of these activities, students will be able to:

- *Meet standards:* The scientific method allows for meaningful questions while conducting careful investigations. As a basis for understanding photosynthesis and transpiration students should develop their own questions and perform investigations by
  1. Observing the effect of light on plants and being able to explain the effect of photosynthesis
  2. Demonstrating their understanding of how green plants use the sun's energy to produce food through photosynthesis
  3. Being able to prove that plants are part of many natural cycles

MATERIALS AND TOOLS

- Two or more 6-inch pots
- 50 or more pea seeds
- Vermiculture soil mix (or potting soil)
- A sprinkler (a jar with holes in the lid)
- A dark area (a large cardboard box) or a cabinet
- A glass bottle or jar
- Paper
- Pencils
- Crayons.

ELL Adaptation: The teacher writes on the chalkboard or shows a poster with words related to the lesson topic and explains their meaning. Illustrations can be helpful. The teacher reads each word aloud and asks students to repeat them in chorus. Students may write their first-language equivalents together with new words in their vocabulary list or in a notebook.

PROCEDURES

Introduction (5 min.): The teacher will ask students questions about photosynthesis and transpiration using samples from real life.

Presentation (15 min.): The teacher will read a short lecture about plants that provide renewable sources of food energy for many forms of life. Green plants use the sun's energy and the gases in the atmosphere to produce food through photosynthesis and exchange gases in the atmosphere in the associated process of transpiration. A video about photosynthesis and transpiration would be very appropriate.

Activities (24 min.): This assignment should be given three or four days before the lesson. Germinate pea seeds by placing them on damp paper towels in a tray or shallow dish and covering them with warm tap water. Keep covered with warm water and in an indirectly lit place. A "hook" should appear in two to three days. After the "hook" appears, the seeds are ready to be planted in the pots.

Prepare two pots by placing paper towels as a lining for each pot. Fill with the vermiculite soil mixture up to 2½ inches from the top. Place the seeds carefully on top of mixture. Cover with ¼ to ½ inches of soil mix. Sprinkle water over the top of the soil until the soil is well saturated. Place one of the pots in a well-lit place. Place the other pot in the designated dark area and leave it completely in the dark for one week to ten days.

At the end of one week or ten days, remove the pot from the designated dark area and compare it with the pot of seedlings that were grown in the light. Have the class discuss the differences and make a drawing to illustrate the differences between the two sets of seedlings. Leave the pot that was in the dark in the light for a few days and compare the results. Remove one seedling from each pot and compare the root structure of the dark-grown seedlings and the light grown seedlings. Place a glass bottle over one of the seedlings and place it in the sunlight. Notice the condensation that occurs on the inside of the bottle. The condensation is water vapor being given off by the plant when it exchanges oxygen for carbon dioxide (transpiration).

1. Divide the class into groups of three (if not conducting this experiment as a demo.) Have each student make an illustrated log of events from germination of the seedings to the end of the experiment. Ask students to share and discuss their findings.

2. Suggest that students in groups of four develop a detailed instruction on how to conduct this experiment.

Field Study Extensions

1. Take the class out to a grassy area on the school grounds. Dig up a shovelful of grass-covered soil. Have the class examine and discuss the depth of the roots and their structure. For example, how do they differ from the pea seedling roots? How does grass differ physiologically from the pea seedlings (stems, leaves, and the like)? Do they have the same photosynthetic process?

2. Take the class to a forested area. Compare the effect of light on identical seedlings growing in the shade of a tree and seedlings growing in sunlight. Write a report on the effects of photosynthesis and transpiration based on observation.

REFLECTIVE ASSESSMENT AND EVALUATIONS

Students will be assessed in the process of the lesson and evaluated on their completion of the assignments. Students may want to provide their own video clips of their assignments or drawings with written notes.

Homework (**2 min.**): Part of the activities described in the plan should be done as homework. Students are encouraged to explain photosynthesis and transpiration to their parents. Parents should monitor assignments at home.

Closure (**4 min.**): Overview the lesson and ask students explain the two processes, photosynthesis and transpiration.

Lesson Plan 9

LESSON DESCRIPTION

Content Area: Social Studies

Title: How a bill becomes a law

Grade Level: 6–9 (intermediate to secondary)

Author: Adapted from: Wanda Kehl, Desert Shadows Middle School, Scottsdale, Arizona

Rationale: Since early in the 1600s, this land has been the new destination for people from all over the world. These immigrants came to this land for various reasons, some for wealth, some to escape persecution from a king, some for religious freedom, and still more for adventure. All these people came to this land with many hopes, dreams, and visions that eventually led to the forming of a new country, and, in 1788, a new form of government. In the 1800s a great migration of people flooded the United States, expanding our population but also bringing with them their different cultures and value systems. They came to the United States to participate in a unique form of government—not a government of kings or queens, but a government in which they could enter into and play a major part. Thus the people of the United States participate in a government of the people, by the people, and for the people that assures us of certain rights.

GOALS

Students will visualize the step-by-step process of how a bill becomes a law and how involved the process is and participate in the process of writing a proposed law.

OBJECTIVES

As a result of these activities, students will be able to:

- *Meet standards:* Explain the process through which an idea transforms into a bill which in turn can become a law by
  1. Listing the steps needed to move from bill to law
  2. Explaining the three actions the president may take
  3. Describing an override of the president's veto
  4. Arranging the bill to law steps on a poster

MATERIALS AND TOOLS

- Simplified list of the steps of a bill
- 8" × 24" paper
- Ruler
- Colored paper
- Markers
- Video on how a bill becomes a law

ELL Adaptation: The teacher writes on the chalkboard or shows a poster with words related to legal content area and explains their meaning. Students may write their first-language equivalents together with new words in their vocabulary list or notebook.

PROCEDURES

Introduction (3 min.): The teacher will briefly talk about law, what it is and why we need laws.

Presentation (10 min.): The teacher will point out that anyone can come up with an idea for a law. It is the legislative branch that under the state and federal constitutions creates the law. A video about how a bill becomes a law would be very appropriate.

Activities (29 min.):

1. Have students make a list of the bill to law steps. Using their textbook, write out the three actions the president may take and explain each. Describe the term *override* orally
2. In pairs, have students decide on a motif or theme for their poster; create a poster by arranging the motif or theme to illustrate the steps of a bill to become a law.
3. Make a stack of cards with one step written on each card; give one card to different students; have students arrange themselves in the proper order.

4. Suggest that students write a law on environment protection and present it to the class.

REFLECTIVE ASSESSMENT AND EVALUATION

- Assess student work by giving students a step and having them give the next one in proper sequence to another student.
- Collect and grade completed posters.

Homework (2 min.): Ask students to decide what new law the society needs and write a draft of this law. Involve parents by having students share their ideas about needed societal reforms via the law.

Closure (6 min.): Highlight the laws the students have come up with and ask them whom they should contact in the legislature to see if their ideas can one day become a reality.

Lesson Plan 10

LESSON DESCRIPTION

Content Area: Art and language arts

Title: Monochromatic Painting

Grade Level: 5–12 (intermediate to secondary)

Author: Adapted from: Marcella Embry, Washoe County GT, Nevada

Rationale: Students need a better understanding of art and language. This lesson serves the goal and is very simple to prepare; it requires only that the students have access to a sink.

GOALS

The goal of this lesson is to create a connection between art and language and generate critical discussion.

OBJECTIVES

As a result of these activities, students will be able to:
- *Meet standards:* Use the principles of design to create, discuss, analyze, and write about visual aspects of their work and articulate the process and the meaning of color for revising and reworking their own works of art by
  1. Experimenting with monochromatic painting
  2. Creating an original monochromatic painting
  3. Giving definitions of *monochromatic, tint,* and *shade*
  4. Analyzing and evaluating their paintings objectively
  5. Determining the connection between color and emotion

MATERIALS AND TOOLS

- White art paper (either 9 × 12 or 12 × 18)
- Undiluted tempera paint, multiple colors
- Paint brushes, multiple brush sizes
- Paint palettes (can use plastic plates)
- Containers of water (to rinse brushes)
- Rulers, compasses, protractors, pencils
- Reproductions of paintings

ELL Adaptation: The teacher writes on the chalkboard or shows a poster with new words and explains their meaning. Pictures or objects illustrating these words can be helpful. The teacher reads each word aloud and asks students repeat them in chorus. Students may write their first-language equivalents together with new words in their vocabulary list or notebook.

Vocabulary:

1. *Tint:* Adding white to a color to create different hues
2. *Shading:* Adding black to a color to create different hues
3. *Monochromatic:* Artwork created using one color
4. *Palette:* A flat piece of wood or plastic on which an artist mixes colors for painting

PROCEDURES

Introduction (5 min.): The teacher will ask students questions about painting, inviting them to talk about their own experiences. What are the types of paintings, what materials do artists use, where do they get ideas about painting? Have you painted a picture?

Presentation (8 min.): The teacher will give a short lecture about painting, illustrating the talk with pictures. Copies of different paintings will be handy.

Activities (30 min.): Have students close their eyes and imagine that they are either flying or sailing through the Bermuda Triangle. It is a beautiful day without a cloud in the sky. Decide what color would best describe how you feel right now.

As you continue to travel through the Bermuda Triangle, you begin to feel uncomfortable, a little apprehensive. Something is not quite right. What color is this feeling?

Suddenly you see it. It is the scariest thing you've ever seen. What color is this emotion?

Explain to the students that they will be making a monochromatic painting today using one of the colors that described their feeling as they journeyed through the Bermuda Triangle. Demonstrate how different hues are made from color by adding different quantities of white (tinting) or black (shading). Place a small amount of a color of paint on your palette. Mix in a small amount of white paint. Do the same thing, only adding more white (tint) to your color. Make several hues with your color and black (shade).

Give each student a piece of paper, his or her choice of one color of paint, white and black paint, a palette, and a brush. Have the students create large overlapping geometric shapes and fill them in with their new hues using different brushes. Have the students cover the paper completely with the new hues.

After that, students will discuss:

1. How they created certain hues
2. What their impressions were of monochromatic painting
3. How color can be used to portray emotion
4. What they might do differently next time

REFLECTIVE ASSESSMENT AND EVALUATION

Students will demonstrate their paintings and explain the ideas behind them. They will be assessed and evaluated based on their performance and discussion of their work.

Homework (2 min.): Have students bring their works of art home where they will explain the work of art to their parents and get feedback. Students will share these impression with the class.

Closure (5 min.): Ask students to identify various principles of design to create art. Discuss visual aspects and the meaning of color.

Lesson Plan 11

LESSON DESCRIPTION

Content Area: Language arts

Title: Spotting Details

Grade Level: 9–12 (secondary)

Author: Adapted from: Bill Zook, Pine Hills School, Montana

Rationale: This lesson is aimed at developing victim awareness.

GOAL

While the guise of the lesson is creative writing, the subject can be construed to apply to being a witness, and ultimately to a better understanding of why different people report the same event differently.

OBJECTIVES

As a result of these activities, students will be able to:

- *Meet standards:* Verify and clarify facts presented via observation by using one's perspective; make warranted and reasonable assertions about what was seen and defend and clarify interpretations by

  1. Demonstrating the ability to pay closer attention to details and subtleties
  2. Describing details of situations
  3. Explaining perspective

MATERIALS AND TOOLS

- Pencil
- Paper
- A video clip with a situation

  (If no window or street is available, a contrived exhibit could be developed)

ELL Adaptation: The teacher writes on the chalkboard or shows a poster with new words and explains their meaning. Pictures illustrating these words can be helpful. The teacher reads each word aloud and asks students to repeat them in chorus. Students may write their first-language equivalents together with new words in their vocabulary list or notebook.

PROCEDURES (22 min)

Introduction (**4 min.**): The teacher will show students some objects on the table for 30 seconds and then will ask them to enumerate all of them and point to their relative position.

Presentation (**6 min.**): The teacher will read a short lecture about the need for attentive observation and techniques of better attention to details and subtleties.

Activities (**12 min.**):

1. Individually, students are asked to observe changing objects—in this case, the cars passing on the street—for a limited time (2–3 min.). No discussion is permitted until the lesson is completed. On cue, the students return to their desks and record details of items (vehicles) observed and the proper sequence of appearance.
2. Reports are collected and read back to class. These are compared with either a video taken on that occasion—if possible, do it discreetly—or with documentation recorded by instructor.
3. Students discuss what was actually seen and how perspectives can change.
4. A similar assignment will be given to groups of four to five students.

REFLECTIVE ASSESSMENT AND EVALUATION

Students will be assessed in the process of their work and evaluated on their completion of the assignments.

Homework (10 min.): Show students a video clip and ask them to write a detailed description of what they saw. Parents can become part of the process by monitoring the completion of the assignment.

Closure (8 min.): Ask students to identify various techniques of attentive observation and reporting.

Lesson Plan 12

LESSON DESCRIPTION

Content Area: Math

Title: World Population Study

Grade Level: 7–12 (intermediate to secondary)

Author: Adapted from: Margaret V. Smith, Reg. II Observation & Assessment Center, Salt Lake City, Utah

Rationale: This lesson is designed for students of grade levels 7 to 12 who have mastered basic math concepts or can use a calculator to do basic calculations. This lesson is relevant in math, biological and physical sciences, global studies, and current events subject areas. The concept of exponential (as opposed to linear) relationships is a difficult idea for many students to understand. This lesson helps students comprehend the difference between the two and relates this knowledge to human population growth over time.

GOAL

The goal of this lesson is to help students learn about an exponential relationship and how it relates to human population growth and the current global population trends. Students will learn how to graph both exponential and linear information.

OBJECTIVES

As a result of these activities, students will be able to:
- *Meet standards:* Explain exponential function; a function commonly used to study growth and decay. It has the form $y = a^x$ with a positive. Explain linear expression; an expression of the form $ax + b$ where x is variable and a and b are constants; or in more variables, an expression of the form $ax + by + c$, $ax + by + cz + d$, and so on. Demonstrate applications by
  1. Solving a real-life math problem involving multiple and sequential steps to answer a question.

2. Graphing the results of their problem solving to give a visual representation of the results.

3. Explaining the difference between a linear and an exponential relationship.

4. Applying this knowledge to a study of world population growth by making a graph of world population data from 1650 to 2010 (projected).

5. Explaining some of the reasons for the growth in the world's population.

MATERIALS AND TOOLS

- Graph paper
- Pencils
- Rulers
- Calculators
- Blackboard and chalk
- Computer

ELL Adaptation: The teacher writes on the chalkboard or shows a poster with new math terms and explains their meaning. The teacher reads each word aloud and asks students to repeat them in chorus. Students may write their first-language equivalents together with new words in their vocabulary list or notebook.

PROCEDURES

Introduction (3 min.): The teacher will ask students questions about population growth.

Presentation (6 min.): The teacher will give a short lecture about population. The numbers of children "multiply" in each generation. For family B, there are twice as many children each generation, and for family D, there are four times as many. Few families really have the same number of children each generation. But these examples help explain one reason why the world's population has grown rapidly in the last 100 years.

Another reason is that, in most areas of the world, people are living longer. Up until 125 years ago, the world's population was increasing slowly. Although the number of births multiplied, many babies did not live, and large numbers of children and adults died from diseases. Over the past 150 years diet, nutrition, and health care have improved. Scientists have discovered cures for many diseases. As a result, the death rate has been declining rapidly. With more people being born and living longer, the result has been a big jump in the world's population.

There are concerns that, as world population increases, there will be shortages of food and water and the quality of life will be threatened worldwide. What do you think? Discuss and/or debate.

Activities (35 min.):

1. Present the following problem to your students: Imagine you are 4 years old. A rich aunt wants to provide for your future. She has offered to do one of two things.

   Option 1: She would give you $1000 a year until you are 21 (17 years from now); or

   Option 2: She would give you $1 this year, $2 next year, and so on, doubling the amount each year until you were 21.

   Which would you choose? Why? Which way would you have the most money when you were 21?

2. After checking your results with your teacher, get some graph paper and a ruler. Put money on the left, vertical margin, using units of $5000. Put years on the horizontal margin, starting with year 1 to 17 years. Your teacher will demonstrate on the board where to put the information on the graph and how to connect the lines, and you will do this as a class. Find the year along the line at the bottom of the graph and then find the amount of money for that year along the left side of the page. Match up these two amounts and place a dot. When you have placed all your dots, draw a straight, solid line to represent option 1, $1000 per year, and a curved, dotted line to represent option 2, $1 the first year and double that amount every year.

   (If you suspect that the computations part of this problem and the graphing aspects might be too difficult for some of your students, you could pair strong with weaker students or do the entire problem on the board as a class and allow the use of calculators. You could give students an empty, labeled graph if this is new and difficult for them. If some students cannot complete the graph, allow them access to use a completed graph to study.)

3. Study the graph and answer the following questions:
   a. How much money would you have when you were 21 if you chose option 1? How much would you have if you chose option 2?
   b. If you only received money for ten years, which option would give you the most money?
   c. How many years would it be before you had the same amount of money with both options?
   d. Why did the money in option 2 increase so rapidly after the fourteenth year?
   e. Which line do you think would look most like the world's population growth from 1650 to 2010? Why?
   f. Look at the graph. Option 1 represents a simple, direct relationship and is called a linear relationship. Option 2 shows an exponential relationship in which the amount doubles every year. Some exponential relationships increase even more than this. Which option is linear? Which option is exponential?

4. The estimated world population from 1650 to 2000 is listed in the data below. Make your own graph of this information, putting population figures (in millions) on the left vertical margin and years on the horizontal margin. Your teacher will show you an example and help you do this. This line graph will show how fast the world's population is growing. Do you think that a line showing this population growth would look more like the linear or the exponential line from the last exercise? Why?Find the year along the line at the bottom of the graph, and then find the correct population for that year along the left side of the page. With your pencil and ruler, draw one dot for each pair of information. When you have placed all of the dots on the graph, connect them with one curved line.

Year	*World Population* *(in millions, estimated)*
1650	500
1700	600
1750	700
1800	900
1850	1300
1900	1700
1950	2500
1976	4000
2000	7000

Which type of relationship does your graph represent—linear or exponential?

5. To understand why world population is now growing so fast, we will discuss some issues. This activity will help you understand one of them. Read the four "family histories" below and answer the questions. It might be useful to draw a family tree for each one to help you with the math.

Family A: A has one child. If that child has one child, how many grandchildren does A have? If the grandchild has one child, how many great grandchildren does A have?

Family B: B has two children, and each of them has two children. How many grandchildren does B have? If each grandchild has two children, how many great-grandchildren does B have?

Family C: C has three children, and each of them has three children. How many grandchildren does C have? If each grandchild has three children, how many great-grandchildren does C have?

Family D: D has four children, and each of them has four children. How many grandchildren does D have? If each grandchild has four children, how many great-grandchildren does D have?

REFLECTIVE ASSESSMENT AND EVALUATION

Students will be assessed in the process of the lesson, especially in their discussion of the difference between a linear and an exponential relationship, and evaluated on their completion of the assignments.

Homework (3 min.): Draw a genealogy tree of your family, if you can. Comment on the family growth. Parents can help with facts and figures about the family tree. If the data are unavailable, go on the Internet and find three articles on demographics. Make an analytical review of these papers, comparing their data and conclusions.

Closure (3 min.): Overview the lesson and its major ideas with special attention being paid to worldwide population growth.

Lesson Plan 13

LESSON DESCRIPTION

Content Area: Health and consumerism

Title: Comparison Food Shopping: Buying Groceries for Two People for One Week

Grade Level: 9–12 (secondary)

Author: Adapted from: Kay B. Edwards, Marana PLUS Program, Marana Public Schools, Marana, Arizona

Rationale: There is a need for consumer awareness in food consumption.

GOAL

The goal of this lesson is to have students discover that nutritious food can be bought and prepared more cheaply than fast food.

OBJECTIVES

As a result of these activities, students will be able to:

- *Meet standards:* Analyze how to devise a healthy and economical diet via access to information by
  1. Compiling a simple food budget for two
  2. Comparing shops through newspaper and Internet ads
  3. Calculating the calorie content of common foods
  4. Arguing a healthy diet for themselves

MATERIALS AND TOOLS

- Regular notebook paper
- Scissors
- Paste or scotch tape
- Calculator
- Several days' worth of food ads from your local newspaper, along with teacher packet of information on food groups and calories
- Access to the Internet

ELL Adaptation: The teacher writes on the chalkboard or shows a poster with new words and explains their meaning. Pictures illustrating these words can be helpful. The teacher reads each word aloud and asks students to repeat them in chorus. Students may write their first-language equivalents together with new words in their vocabulary list or notebook.

PROCEDURES

Introduction (4 min.): The teacher will ask students questions about food habits and the cost of food.

Presentation (10 min.): The teacher will read a short lecture about healthy food consumption. The teacher will discuss with the students the importance of good diets and of staying within a food budget. This may include asking each student for a favorite food and finding out how many choices are home cooked and how many are fast food. Ask the students if they have any idea how nutritious their favorite food is—or how much of a junk-food item it really is! Other questions could center around how much money is spent on eating out in a typical week and how much of a person's total income can be budgeted for food. It's always interesting to discuss school cafeteria food. (The possibilities are endless.)

Activities (28 min.):

1. Once the presentation is over, divide the class into groups of five and pass out an information packet for this project. Included is a statement of how much money can be spent for food for two people for one week: for example, $100.00. Included also are some pages of information on the basic four food groups and sample calorie amounts for an adult portion of common foods. A lot or a little discussion may be needed at this point, depending on the students' background in food preparation and living on their own. Students are directed to "shop" from the local Wednesday newspapers, since this is the day when the most food ads are included. Each student is to "spend" his or her $100.00 in a way that is nutritious and varied, remembering that he or she is shopping for two.

   Students will survey the ads for the four basic food groups. He or she will look for meat such as frying chickens at 50 cents per pound; bananas at 2 pounds for a dollar; 2 percent milk, $1.99 per gallon, and so on.

Students will keep a running list of money spent. When each has spent approximately $100.00, he or she cuts out the ads and mounts them neatly on notebook paper. The student then double-checks to see that each food group is represented every day in approximately ideal amounts.

After this activity is over, on a separate piece of notebook paper, the student totals his or her purchases to reaffirm that the goal of $100.00 or less has been met.

2. Students will approximate the number of calories for each meal per person, comparing the number of calories to an ideal number for a young, active adult, and adjust accordingly.

3. Students can share their findings. Were they surprised by how expensive food was or how cheap? Did they improve their awareness of calories and menus? Is there money left over for an occasional Big Mac?

4. Enrichment activities include finding or inventing tasty recipes, varying the number of calories consumed to provide a person on a diet to lose weight or to gain weight, or clipping coupons and figuring the savings. A student pamphlet with recipes and accompanying calorie list could be prepared and distributed; an article could be written for the student newspaper, a bulletin board display could be set up in the library. A team of students could analyze the school cafeteria food for a week to determine the number of calories in a typical meal.

REFLECTIVE ASSESSMENT AND EVALUATIONS

Students will be assessed in the process of the lesson and evaluated on their completion of the assignments with special emphasis put on a healthy diet.

Homework **(2 min.):** Prepare a weekly food budget for your family. Let parents know about the project so they can help to make calculations correctly and monitor to be sure the assignment is completed. Calculate the number of calories you consume during the day. Assess your findings and see if you enjoy a healthy diet.

Closure **(6 min.):** Let students discuss the benefits of healthy diet and home budgets and consider lifestyle changes that help their pocketbook and their health.

Lesson Plan 14

LESSON DESCRIPTION

Content Area: Math or science

Title: Improving Deductive Reasoning Skills

Grade Level: 7–12 (secondary)

Author: Paul Allan, Palmer High School, Palmer, Alaska

Rationale: The focus of the lesson is to introduce deductive reasoning. Use Mind Bender puzzles that require little math knowledge to teach cooperative grouping techniques. This technique can be used in heterogeneous groups of four. Student-produced puzzles can earn them extra credit.

GOAL

The goal of this lesson is to enhance student problem-solving capabilities.

OBJECTIVES

As a result of these activities, students will be able to:

- *Meet standards:* Reason deductively in a coherent and focused manner on a variety of problems by
  1. Recognizing problems that may be solved using deductive reasoning
  2. Developing techniques to help them in solving deductive reasoning problems
  3. Solving deductive reasoning problems
  4. Producing their own deductive reasoning puzzles for other students to solve

MATERIALS AND TOOLS

At the beginning of the lesson, use materials from Mind Benders (Midwest Publications Co.) copied onto overheads and "help charts" copied on paper for each group.

ELL Adaptation: The teacher writes on the chalkboard or shows a poster with new words and explains their meaning. Pictures illustrating these words can be helpful. The teacher reads each word aloud and asks students to repeat them in chorus. Students may write their first-language equivalents together with new words in their vocabulary list or notebook.

PROCEDURES

Introduction (3 min.): Students are reminded of the deductive reasoning skills used by Sherlock Holmes to solve his mysteries.

Presentation (6 min.): The teacher should read some excerpts from Sherlock Holmes stories.

Activities (30 min.):

1. Students are divided into small groups and asked to solve deductive reasoning puzzles. After the groups have worked on solving the puzzle, the class should be brought together to discuss the strategies employed to solve the puzzle.
2. Once the most effective strategies have been determined, give the student groups another puzzle.

Note: Over a time period of 30 minutes, give the students puzzles of varying degrees of difficulty. Allow them to use help charts (as provided in the Mind Benders materials) at times but also have them produce their own charts to facilitate their problem solving. The real fun in this lesson starts when the students produce their own puzzles.

They have by now experienced several deductive reasoning puzzles and have seen how the charts can be used as an resource. Ask each student to produce a simple puzzle of his or her own making. The results are really remarkable. Some students start very simply, but then they discover that it is not too hard to make the puzzle special by adding things that are important to them.

Have the students share their puzzles with other students, copying them on overheads for class work or onto paper for individual work. An example of a puzzle produced by a student that is autobiographical follows (the student fits the characteristics of Frank, before he moved to Alaska):

Frank's Puzzle
Don, Frank, Jenny, and Ken each come from one state, either Alaska, Maine, Montana, or Oklahoma. They each speak one primary language, either English, French, Russian, or Spanish. And they each have one of four pets, a chinchilla, a dog, a hamster, or a turtle. To solve this puzzle identify who is who and where each youngster lives using the following information:

1. Frank needed a language book to write to the Alaskan.
2. The youngster from Oklahoma has a mammal for her pet.
3. The Alaskan found his pet outside his door in a snow bank.
4. The French-speaking boy lives east of Oklahoma.
5. The Russian-speaking boy wants to write to the youngster from Montana, but he doesn't speak his language.
6. Don bought his pet in Peru.
7. Ken does not own a hamster.
8. The dog's owner wrote a letter in Russian to the kid in Oklahoma, but she couldn't understand it.
9. Don had to travel west to meet Jenny.
10. Frank is learning Spanish at school.

REFLECTIVE ASSESSMENT AND EVALUATION

Students will be assessed and evaluated based on their problem-solving achievement.

Homework (1 minute): Have students create a new puzzle on their own. Recommend that students explain the puzzles and deductive reasoning to their parents.

Closure (10 min.): Have a general class discussion of the strategies used in solving puzzles. Discuss why deductive reasoning is a useful tool.

Lesson Plan 15

LESSON DESCRIPTION

Content Area: Language arts, social studies

Title: Timelines

Grade Level: All levels

Author: Penny Sexton, Okemah High School, Okemah, Oklahoma

Rationale: This lesson addresses history of the city and state and of a student's life.

GOAL

In finding out the contemporary history at their birth, students discover much about themselves and world in which they live.

OBJECTIVES

As a result of this lesson, students will be able to:

- *Meet standards:* Compare and contrast everyday life in different eras and comprehend that some aspects of people, places, and some things change over time while others remain the same by

  1. Examining their community in the past
  2. Recognizing similarities and differences of earlier generations inside their community
  3. Presenting a completed timeline indicating answers to previously determined questions

MATERIALS AND TOOLS

- Tom Snyder Productions "Timeliner"
- Local newspaper archives

ELL Adaptation: The teacher writes on the chalkboard or shows a poster with new words and explains their meaning. Pictures illustrating these words can be helpful. The teacher reads each word aloud and asks students to repeat them in chorus. Students may write their first-language equivalents together with new words in their vocabulary list or notebook.

PROCEDURES

Introduction (3 min.): The teacher talks about time lines applied to the city in which students live.

Activities (35 min.):

1. In groups of three, students will research the local newspapers' archives (for example, use online resources) on the date of their birth to find the following information which occurred on their birth date:
    *   Major headlines
    *   Prices of products
    *   What movie was showing at the local theater
    *   One birth announcement
    *   One wedding announcement

    Students will develop a time line on the computer to present research information.

2. Time lines should be placed in classrooms for viewing and discussion. This lesson can be used for ESL classes.

REFLECTIVE ASSESSMENT AND EVALUATION

Students will present their findings. They will be assessed and evaluated based on their performance, posters, and discussion of their work.

Homework (2 min.): Have students bring their time lines home where they will explain them to their parents and ask for their input. They will share their parents' information in the next lesson.

Closure (10 min.): Ask students to discuss various time lines and their importance in their lives.

APPENDIX E

5-Star Lesson Plan Worksheet

1. DESCRIPTION

Date: _____

Subject: _____

Topic: _____

Grade: _____

2. GOALS AND OBJECTIVES

Goals: _____

_____

_____

Objectives: _____

_____

_____

Standards: _____

_____

_____

Accommodations for ELL/ SDAIE: _____

_____

_____

Basic Vocabulary: _____

_____

_____

3. MATERIALS AND TOOLS

Texts: _____

_____

Visuals: _____

_____

Technologies: _____

_____

Handouts: _____

_____

4. PROCEDURE

Introduction (_____ *min.):* _____

_____

_____

Teacher Presentation (_____ *min.):* _____

_____

_____

Class Activities (_____ *min.):* _____

_____

_____

Homework (_____ *min.):* _____

_____

_____

Closure (_____ min.): _____

_____

_____

5. REFLECTIVE ASSESSMENT AND/OR EVALUATION

Conferences: _____

_____

_____

Testing: _____

_____

_____

GLOSSARY

Accommodation This concept helps ensure the learning process for every student. The authors use the most encompassing view of the notion of inclusion to cover all students. It includes content adaptation; special strategies, such as vocabulary; work before new material presentation to help ELL and special needs students; slow but natural speech; clear enunciation; short, simple sentences; visual reinforcement; and frequent comprehension checks.

Activity This concept functions to implement a strategy. A strategy in action is an activity. Activities are student actions targeting certain knowledge and skills. For example, listening, speaking, reading, writing, dancing, and singing can all be activities that advance a given conceptual strategy.

Affective domain This realm of learning involves our emotions and values. Inspiration, motivation and empowerment, all affective in nature, express our deepest feelings of self-worth and commitment. One's affective disposition is interwoven into one's cognitive ability. A teacher's natural disposition, supportive and caring attitude towards students, positive environment, music, visuals, and the environment of joy and achievement are some of the affective factors.

Algorithm A procedure consisting of a finite set of predetermined instructions desined to accomplish a given task, which will lead to a predefined outcome. Algorithms often have steps that repeat (iterate) or require making decisions using the "If . . . then . . ." logical formula. There are three basic forms of an algorithm: linear, branching, or iterative. A lesson plan can be presented as an algorithm as it moves step-by-step from one activity to another.

Assessment An appraisal of the learner that is inherently reflective, which is derived from the Latin *assidere*, which literally means, "to sit beside." If one can imagine an examiner sitting alongside a student and providing feedback (based on observing, documenting, and analyzing the learner's work), we can better understand how the student is to accomplish genuine *assessment*, which is, in fact, self-*assessment*.

Asynchronous learning (design) Learning opportunities and support free of time constraints. It often exists in a self-learning mode or in web-based education. Threaded discussion in an online class is an example of asynchronous design.

Basic vocabulary A minimal set of words necessary for student to understand a particular topic. New information can be made meaningful to every student by defining ideas and activities using a fundamental terminology that is a part of basic vocabulary.

Classroom activities These behaviors make up the phase when students perform various assignments, individual or collaborative, among which are: problem-solving, case studies, discussions, exercises, role playing, experimenting, and presenting. These activities may be of at least two levels of complexity: basic (guided exercises) and advanced (independent practice).

Class section A subdivision of a course populated with a finite number of students that begins with the preview of the new plan and ends with the reflective review of the most important items.

Closure A phase that incorporates the review of the lesson and the summary of the lesson's key points. It usually follows general appraisal (assessment and evaluation) of the students' work and can include a short preview of the lesson to come.

Constructivism A learning theory based on the notion of building up one's own knowledge via the interaction between prior knowledge and new knowledge. Most effective knowledge is constructed in collaboration with peers under the guidance of an expert (teacher).

Course A learning entity that delivers a certain subject matter or specific content representing a particular area that can be considered as a whole. Usually taught over an extended period of time (a semester or a school year).

Curriculum   The concept of what is to be taught to prepare students for a given purpose that lays a foundation of the educational program. It has structure and contains content areas that are interrelated and interdependent.

Discipline   An educational subject matter division (e.g. history, science, foreign language) that starts with the introduction previewing its structure, content, activities and outcomes.

Educational technology (ET)   Technical, programming, and instructional tools used together with human resources in teaching and learning.

ELL   English language learner; a student whose first language is other than English.

Email   A communication tool for individual and group message exchange. At the same time, it is a great instrument for reading and writing instruction, individual and group tutoring and consultations, question and answer exercises, problem solving and role playing.

Evaluation   A one-time glimpse of a student's knowledge expressed in a score, ranking, or grade that exists at a given point in time.

5-Star Lesson Plan   An organized methodological approach for lesson planning that contains distinct components including (1) lesson description, (2) goals and objectives, (3) materials and tools, (4) procedure, (5) reflective assessment and evaluation.

Gestalt   An overview based on a holistic organizing principle or pattern.

Goal   This concept represents a strategic, ultimate aim or purpose as given in the lesson.

Grade (level of learning)   A hierarchical system based on student merit to move from a lower level to a higher level in school based on a combination of prior knowledge, mastery of specific curricular content, and to some extent the student's age.

Grade (score)   A quantitative measure usually communicated via a letter (e.g., A, B, C, D, F) or a numerical evaluation (e.g. 75%), or a numerical score (e.g., 1-5).

Handouts   Tangible material given to students that can extend on or enhance the curriculum.

Homework   An extension of the school day via home study, vital for providing further independent learning, real-life applications and experiences, and for assuring retention.

Homework checkup   A stage in the class during which the students present their assigned out-of-class work, either by making oral presentations or by turning in written work. It is important that the students realize that "we don't do disposable work."

Instructional tool   This represents anything that facilitates teaching and learning. We know that a fork or chopsticks are tools for eating. A book, felt-tip marker, computer, or software program are all examples of instructional tools.

Introduction   The initial part or phase of the lesson, intended to prepare students for learning by warming up, general conversation, reviewing the previous lesson's key points, setting the objectives and presenting the plan of the current lesson, and doing preliminary exercises.

Iteration   A repeated procedure intended to bring student competence to a predetermined level of learning outcomes.

Lesson plan   A systemic, research-based sequence of instructional events to be implemented in a future lesson. It is the foundation of successful student learning, accurate assessment, and effective classroom management. It is essential in almost any aspect of daily classroom life.

Lesson plan description   A formal part of the lesson plan containing all the essential information about lesson plan: the date of the lesson, the topic, subject area, grade, goals and objectives, standards, and rationale.

Lesson planning   A regular teacher activity intended to prepare quality instruction. This helps to structure instruction, learning, classroom practice, and teacher time. This eventually makes your teaching performance more efficient, less stressful and, which is crucial, rewarding for you. Most importantly, a well-constructed lesson plan sets a pathway to learning for your students.

Lessons in a course   The constituent parts of a course, each of them being derived from another and dependent on the others. In the instructional process they extend sequentially through a certain period of time (a year, a semester, a quarter, a month, a week, or a day) and together form a complete single whole, both as a system and as a continuum.

Manipulatives   Items to aid the learning process. For example, they may include objects commonly used to build structures, as with blocks; to test recollection, as with flash cards; or to count up tangible sums, as with beans.

Materials   Anything carrying information or used for constructing knowledge and developing skills, including texts or any other reading materials; visuals, such as drawings, pictures, posters, or handouts; as well as realia and materials for drawing, coloring, constructing, such as paper, clay, fabric, cardboard, etc.

Method   A concept that represents a theoretical instructional approach. For example, one can practice the communicative approach, accelerated learning, or cooperative learning. All are considered methodological in nature.

Modeling   Also *simulation,* is another side of organizating and structuring. When you prepare a lesson, you actually create a lesson prototype, an organizational structure of the instructional process you are going to implement in your class. If you look at the lesson plan you have just developed from this perspective, you will realize that it is actually a model of your future lesson (Serdyukov 2002). It will prescribe the what, how, when and time allotted to structured classroom activities.

Motivation   It is a driving force in student learning that is closely connected to the affective domain. Two types of motivation are known: extrinsic and intrinsic, the latter being the more efficient and more powerful of the two because it resides in the learner. To have a student increase his or her motivation for learning, resulting in enhanced achievement, it is imperative for the teacher to set an environment where the learner elects to become engaged in culturally responsive goals and objectives that are personally important to the student.

Objective   A concept that represents one of the specific, explicit, intermediate aims that help achieve pre-designed outcomes of the lesson. The objectives for the lesson plan are determined by the broader goals of the lesson.

Organized learning   This requires planning, and the latter is the foundation of education. Creating a lesson plan involves planning for learning experiences.

Outcomes   The implemented objectives achieved through effective instruction and students' learning.

Plan   A systematic means to reach an end.

Presentation   The phase of the lesson when new material is introduced by the teacher in the form of an expository lecture or a narrative, or by reading from a text. Often the teacher uses various visuals germane to the area of study.

Prior knowledge   The understanding that students bring to classroom. New knowledge begins to be understood when the learner uses his or her prior knowledge to make out familiar patterns of thought within the new knowledge in order to interpret new or enhanced meanings. Within the constructivist framework, prior knowledge is a significant factor in the learning process.

Procedure   A critical part of any lesson, where the teacher and students interact and communicate, share information, solve problems and do assignments to achieve the lesson goals and objectives. It is through procedures that knowledge is constructed and retained, and skills are developed and applied.

Professional competence The ability to efficiently perform on the job.

Realia Various real-life objects that help make learning more realistic. They may include, for instance, price lists from stores that can be used in home economics class, menus from restaurants in an ESL lesson on food and eating, a collection of stones in a science lesson on earth and geology, chemical substances for chemistry experiments.

SDAIE (Specially Designed Academic Instruction in English) A methodologically organized set of effective transitional strategies and best practices that provide an instructional model for a linguistically diverse classroom. This specific method emanates from learning theory based on the notions of "comprehensible second language input" and a "supportive affective environment". SDAIE methodology permits students to engage in academic courses such as math and science while simultaneously, via contextual clues within the course, learning English.

Socratic seminar A method to move from the unexamined to the examined by participating in a dialogue about a specific idea or text. Thoughtful conversation is dependent on higher order critical thinking in the search for meaning rather than regurgitation of information.

Space Physical space or area where learning takes place: a classroom, laboratory, or playground.

Spiral curriculum This is an evolutionary concept beginning with a foundational notion that develops new yet connected knowledge via repetitive procedures culminating in covering the entire curriculum.

Standard Identified subject area content, which should be aligned with test content. Academic standards define both breadth and depth. State standards typically delineate anticipated outcomes. In simple terms they state what students are required to know and what students should be able to perform.

Strategic planning Designing a course in a particular subject area (the principles and rules of which are dealt with in the theory of Instructional Design).

Strategy Particular implementation of a method that operates through specially organized instructional activities.

Structured classroom activity This is a major element of your plan and a basic unit of organized learning.

Subject a learning discipline, or a content area (e.g. math, science, history, fine arts).

Tactical planning Daily instruction design focusing on immediate tasks.

Technology Electronic and mechanical devices that can produce and project images and sounds, create and save textual, visual and audio information, used as a tool in the classroom. For example, the computer and the Internet represent learning tools as we look through a display window to the world in our journey through cyberspace.

Technology applications Special instructional uses of technology in teaching and learning.

Time A most significant commodity for a teacher and for a learner because it demands changes in curricular and methodological considerations. These changes affect your lesson plan.

Tools The teacher's and student's instruments that can be non-technological, such as chalk board, ruler, textbooks, dictionaries, reference books, or technological, based on electronics, mechanics, and optics, such as computers, calculators, DVD players, overhead projectors, computer programs, and Internet.

Topic A particular curricular focus within the lesson description component of a lesson plan (e.g. "Reasons for the American Revolution" in a United States history class, or how to calculate percents in a math class.)

SUGGESTED READINGS

Aronson, J. (ed.). (2002). *Improving academic achievement: Impact of psychological factors on education.* Boston: Academic Press.

Barkley, S. (1999) Time: It's made, not found. *J. of Staff development,* Fall 1999, v. 20, No. 4.

Bloom, B., Engelhart, M., Furst, E., Hill, W. & Krathwohl, D. (1956). *Taxonomy of educational objectives: cognitive domain.* New York: Longman

Bloom, B. S. (1980). The new direction in educational research: alterable variables. *Phi Delta Kappan, 61 (6),* 382-385.

Bloom's Taxonomy: http://www.coun.uvic.ca/learn/program/hndouts/bloom.html

Bowling, N., Ries, K & Ivanitskaya L. (2002). How effective are compressed courses? *On Target, 1(3)* 2002. Retrieved on 11/06/06 from http://www.cel.cmich.edu/ontarget/aug02/

Boyes, L., Reid, I., Brain, K. and Wilson, J. (2004). *Accelerated learning: a literature survey.* Unit for Educational Research & Evaluation, University of Bradford. http://www.standards.dfes.gov.uk/giftedandtalented/downloads/word/ accellearnreport.doc

Boyle-Baise, M. (2002). *Multicultural service learning: Educating teachers in diverse communities.* New York: Teachers College Press.

Buchler, B. (2003). Critical issue: terms of engagement—rethinking teachers' independent learning traits. http://www.ncrel.org/sdrs/areas/issues/educatrs/ profdevl/pd400.htm

Burnette, J. (1999). Critical behaviors and strategies for teaching culturally diverse students. ERIC/OSEP Digest.

Chall, J. S. (2000). *The academic achievement challenge: What really works in the classroom?* New York: Guilford Press.

Christenson, S. L., & Sheridan, S. M. (2001). *Schools and families: Creating essential connections for learning.* New York: Guilford Press.

Christison, M.; Kennedy, D. (1999). Multiple intelligences: Theory and practice in adult ESL, ERIC Digest.

Cotton, K. (2000). *The schooling practices that matter most.* Alexandria, VA: Association for Supervision and Curriculum Development.

Cummins, J. (1979) Cognitive/academic language proficiency, linguistic interdependence, the optimum age question and some other matters. *Working papers on bilingualism,* No. 19, 121–129.

Davis-Johnson, S. P. (2001). *7 essentials for character discipline: Elementary classroom management.* Thousand Oaks, CA: Corwin Press.

Dewey, J. (1938). *Experience and education.* New York: Macmillan.

Eggen, P. D., Kauchak, D. P. (2006). *Learning and teaching research-based methods.* Boston: Allyn and Bacon.

Ellison, L. (2001). *The personal intelligences: Promoting social and emotional learning.* Thousand Oaks, CA: Corwin Press.

Engels, F. (1987). Anti-Duhring. In *Marx-Engels collected works,* Vol, 25. New York: International Publishers.

Fuchs, L. S., Fuchs, D., Karns, K., Hamlett, C. L., Katzaroff, M., and Dutka, S., (1997) Effects of task-focused goals on low-achieving students without learning disabilities. *American Educational Research Journal 34* (3) 513–543.

Gardner, H. (1993). *Frames of mind: The theory of multiple intelligences.* (10th ed.). New York: Basic Books.

Gildner, C. (2001). *Enjoy teaching: Helpful hints for the classroom.* Lanham, MD: Scarecrow Education.

Greiner, C., Serdyukova, N., Subbotin, I. & Serdyukov, P. (2005). A changing paradigm of adult learning: Accessible, accelerated, adaptable, applicable. *Proceedings of the WCCE 2005 World Conference on Computers in Education,* Cape Town, July 2005.

Gronlund, N. E. (2000) *Writing instructional objectives for teaching and assessment.* (7th ed.) Upper Saddle River, NJ: Merrill/Prentice Hall.

Harlan, J. C., & Rowland, S. T. (2002). *Behavior management strategies for teachers: Achieving instructional effectiveness, student success, and student motivation—every teacher and any student can.* Springfield, IL: Charles C. Thomas.

Hebert, E. A. (2001). *The power of portfolios: What children can teach us about learning and assessment.* San Francisco: Jossey-Bass.

Henze, R. (2002). *Leading for diversity: How school leaders promote positive interethnic relations.* Thousand Oaks, CA: Corwin Press.

Hopkins, D. (2001). *School improvement for real.* New York: Routledge.

Hunter, M. (1995). Mastery teaching. Thousand Oaks: Corwin Press, Inc.

Joyce, B., & Weil, M. with Calhoun, E. (2004). *Models of teaching* (7th ed.) Boston: Allyn and Bacon.

Kane, C. (1994) *Prisoners of time.* Report of the National Education Commission on Time and Learning. April 1994 http://ed.gov/pubs/PrisonersOfTime/Prisoners.html

Kitaigorodskaya, G. (1995). *Intensive foreign language training: History, current status and future trends.* Moscow: MGU.

Kleinert, H. L., & Kearns, J. (2001). *Alternate assessment: Measuring outcomes and supports for students with disabilities.* Baltimore, MD: P. H. Brookes Pub. Co.

Knowles, M. (1975). *Self-directed learning: A guide for learners and teachers.* New York: Association Press.

Kuh, G., Kinzie, J., Schuh, J. Whitt, E. et al. (2005). *Student success in college.* San Francisco: Jossey-Bass, A Wiley Imprint.

Lasley, T. J., Matczynski, T. J., & Rowley, J. (2002). *Instructional models: Strategies for teaching in a diverse society.* Belmont, CA: Wadsworth/ Thomson Learning.

Levin, B. (2001). *Reforming education: From origins to outcomes.* New York: Routledge/Falmer.

Lozanov, G. (1978). *Suggestology and outlines of suggestopedy.* New York: Gordon and Breach Science Pub.

Mager, R. (1962). *Preparing instructional objectives.* Palo Alto: Fearon Publishers, Inc.

Marjoribanks, K. (2002). *Family and school capital: Towards a context theory of students' school outcomes.* Boston: Kluwer Academic Publishers.

McMillan, J. H. (2001). *Classroom assessment: Principles and practice for effective instruction.* Boston: Allyn and Bacon.

Metzker, B. (2003) Time and learning. *ERIC Digest* ED474260 http://eric.ed.gov/

Midgley, C. (ed.). (2002). *Goals, goal structures, and patterns of adaptive learning.* Mahwah, NJ: Lawrence Erlbaum.

Mora, J.K. Effective lesson planning for English language learners. San Diego State University http://coe.sdsu.edu/people/jmora/ MoraModules/ELLInstruction.htm# LessonPlan

Naparstek, N. (2002). *Successful educators: A practical guide for understanding children's learning problems and mental health issues.* Westport, CT: Bergin & Garvey.

Ngeow, K. Y. (1999). Online resources for parent/family involvement. *ERIC Clearinghouse on Reading, English, and Communication.* Bloomington IN. [ED432775]

Oakes J. (1985). *Keeping track, how schools structure inequality.* New Haven: Yale University Press.

Orlich, D.C., Harder, R.J., Callahan, R.C., Gibson, H.W. (2001). *Teaching strategies: A guide to better instruction.* Boston: Houghton Mifflin Company.

Parsons, B. A. (2002). *Evaluative inquiry: Using evaluation to promote student success.* Thousand Oaks, CA: Corwin Press.

Queen, J. A. (2003). *The block scheduling handbook.* Thousand Oaks, CA: Corwin Press.

Rauscher, F. H., Shaw, G. L, & Ky, K. N. (1993). Music and spatial task performance. *Nature, 365,* 611.

Rumble, G. (2001). The costs and costing of networked learning. *JALN* Volume 5, Issue 2, September 2001 http://sloan-c.org/ publications/jaln/v5n2/pdf/v5n2_ rumble. pdf

Ryan, M. (1991). Intensive learning: An answer to the dropout crisis, *NASSP Bulletin,* 75 (538), 25–30.

Ryan, M. (2007). *Ask the teacher: A practitioner's guide to teaching and learning in the diverse classroom.* Boston, MA: Allyn and Bacon

Schwartz, P., & Webb, G. (Eds.). (2002). *Assessment: Case studies, experience and practice.* London: Kogan Page.

Scott, P. & Conrad, C. (1992). A critique of intensive courses and an agenda for research. *Higher education: Handbook of theory and research. New York:* Agathod Press.

Serdyukov, P. (1984). *Fundamentals of intensive foreign language instruction.* Kiev: Vystcha Shkola.

Serdyukov, P. (2002) *Lesson plan: A teacher's guide.* Boston: Pearson Education.

Serdyukov, P. (2005) Effective lesson planning. In: Lessow-Hurley, J. (2005). *The foundations of dual language instruction* (4th ed.). With Serdyukov, P. (2004). *Effective lesson planning.* (3rd ed.) Boston: Addison Wesley Longman, Inc.

Serdyukov, P., and Hill, R. (2004). Masonry of E-learning: Managing Knowledge Construction and Skill Development in an Online Course. *Proceedings of E-Learn World Conference on E-Learning in Corporate, Government, Healthcare, & Higher Education,* Washington, D.C., November 2004

Serdyukov, P. & Serdyukova, N. (2004). Intensive short-term learning: Some approaches to contemporary adult education. *Int. J. Cont. Engineering Education and Lifelong Learning,* 14(1/2), 58–67.

Serdyukov, P. and Serdyukova, N. (2006). Time efficiency of online learning. *Proceedings of The 22nd ICDE World Conference,* September 3–6, 2006 in Rio de Janeiro, Brazil.

Siraj-Blatchford, I., & Clarke, P. (2000). *Supporting identity, diversity, and language in the early years*. Philadelphia, PA: Open University Press.

Slavin, R. E., & Madden, N. A. (Eds.). (2001). *Success for all: Research and reform in elementary education*. Mahwah, NJ: L. Erlbaum Associates.

Stefanakis, E. H. (2002). *Multiple intelligences and portfolios: A window into the learner's mind*. Portsmouth, NH: Heinemann.

Stipek, D., & Seal, K. (2001). *Motivated minds: Raising children to love learning*. New York: H. Holt and Co.

Thompson, W. F., Schellenberg, E. G., & Husain, G. (2001). Arousal, mood, and the Mozart effect. *Psychological Science*, 12 (3), 248–251.

Tyler, R.W. (1949). *Basic principles of curriculum and instruction*. Chicago: University of Chicago Press.

Vygotsky, L.S. (1978). *Mind in society: The development of higher psychological processes* (M. Cole, V. John-Steiner, S. Scribner, & E. Souberman, Eds. and Trans.). Cambridge, MA: Harvard University Press.

Walker, Wilson, L. (2002). *Better instruction through assessment: What your students are trying to tell you*. Larchmont, NY: Eye on Education.

Whitley, M. D. (2001). *Bright minds, poor grades*. New York: Perigee.

York-Barr, J. (2001). *Reflective practice to improve schools: An action guide for educators*. Thousand Oaks, CA: Corwin Pres.

Zimmerman, B. J., & Schunk, D. H. (Eds.). (2001). *Self-regulated learning and academic achievement: Theoretical perspectives*. Mahwah, NJ: Lawrence Erlbaum Associates.

Web Links:

http://ericir.syr.edu/Virtual A library of lesson plans created by teachers

The Gateway to Educational Materials http://www.thegateway.org

Developing Learning Outcomes. http://www.stedwards.edu/cte/learningout.htm

Instructional Planning Template http://wwwbel.lkwash.wednet.edu/NAESP/template.html

Ask ERIC Lesson Plans http://www.askeric.org/Virtual/Lessons/

Busy Teachers' WebSite K–12 http://www.ceismc.gatech.edu/busyt

CEC Lesson Plans http://www.col-ed.org/cur/

CNN/AOL @ School http://school.aol.com/teachers/lessonplans.adp

EdHelper www.edhelper.com/

Education World Lesson Planning Center http://www.education-world.com/alesson/

Effective Lesson Planning for English Language Learners http://coe.sdsu.edu/people/jmora/5StepELL/Default.htm

ENCARTA lesson collection http://encarta.msn.com/schoolhouse/default.asp

English Companion http://www.englishcompanion.com/

ERIC/CLL Language Link http://www.cal.org/ericcll/

LessonPlanners.com http://www.lessonplanners.com/

Lesson Plans and Projects. AOL School http://school.aol.com/teachers/lessonplans.adp

Lesson Plans and Teaching strategies http://www.csun.edu/~hcedu013/plans.html#Lesson%20Plans

Lesson Plans at Teachnet www.teachnet.com/lesson.html

Lesson plans by Gibson Associates http://www.netcore.ca/~gibsonjs/gaweb1.htm

LessonPlansPage.com http://www.lessonplanspage.com/

PBS Teacher Source http://www.pbs.org/teachersource/search.htm

SDAIE Handbook: Techniques, Strategies, and Suggestions for Teachers of LEP and Former LEP Students http://www.csupomona.edu/~tassi/sdaie.htm

Some Basic Lesson Presentation Elements http://www.humboldt.edu/~tha1/hunter-eei.html

Teachers' Net Lesson Bank http://teachers.net/lessons/

Teachers.net http://teachers.net/lessons

TESL-EJ. Teaching English as a Second or Foreign Language. An International Journal. http://www-writing.berkeley.edu/TESL-EJ/index.html

Zoom School http://www.enchantedlearning.com/school/index.shtml

INDEX